What is Tactical Periodization?

Xavier Tamarit

Published by Bennion Kearny Ltd, 2015
Copyright © 2014 MB Football
Original Title: Periodización Táctica
This edition is published by agreement with MB Football
www.mb-football.com

ISBN: 978-1-909125-60-5

Published by Bennion Kearny Limited
6 Woodside
Churnet View Road
Oakamoor
ST10 3AE

www.BennionKearny.com

About this Book

This title is a translation of Xavier Tamarit's book Periodización Táctica. Efforts have been made to remain as faithful to the original text as possible and this can, on occasion, lead to testing sections for the reader. Some content simply does not translate directly nor easily.

In turn, a new Summary section has been added to each chapter that attempts to draw out the primary concepts of the chapter in question.

About The Author

Xavier Tamarit is a professional football coach who made his name at Valencia, in Spain, as the assistant to the head coach Mauricio Pellegrino. During his time there, Tamarit established himself as one of the world's leading experts on Tactical Periodization, and he is currently the assistant coach at Estudiantes de la Plata in Argentina.

About The Translators

Iñaki Samaniego is one of the most upcoming goalkeeper coaches in Europe. Born in Sevilla, and after living and working for several years in England and Holland, he is now back in Spain. Iñaki has coached at important clubs like RCD Espanyol in Barcelona and ADO Den Haag in The Hague. Currently he coaches the goalkeepers of CE Constancia in Mallorca. Besides coaching, Iñaki also gives presentations and practices about goalkeeping, having shared his knowledge about the position in countries like Sweden, Scotland, Holland, England and Spain. Last but not least, Iñaki is also an avid translator, having translated several football related books like the Bestseller Soccer Tough. If you want to know more about him, you can follow him on twitter on @InakiSamaniego

Cecilia Fernandez is an experienced translator and proof-reader, specialising in Spanish and English languages. She studied Media & Communication and she has lived in Latin America and Spain, acquiring a deep understanding of cultural differences and idioms. She is currently based in London, United Kingdom, where she started her own company: Good Words Online (www.goodwordsonline.co.uk).

Table of Contents

Foreword

Football through time, and like many other phenomena created by man, has followed the different paradigms of thinking that respective periods have offered. Football's path has been, and is, motivated by different aspects that interact. It is part of a belief system: a search for the evolution of the game.

In the 'beginning', football was played purely and simply for the pleasure brought about by the activity itself. The quest for victory was part of the essence of the game, but the real pleasure was playing it.

With the need and desire to develop the game, participants started to try and understand how they could improve. Realizing that football was a game that was fundamentally technical, they tried to develop the player technically, with improvements that implied better performances individually and collectively. The way they achieved improvements reflected the scientific paradigm at that time, namely, mechanistic thinking. Different skills were taught and trained separately and, once you mastered them, you would play.

Later on, as things evolved, it was understood that football was not just a technical game, it was also tactical and physical. From that new understanding of the game, the evolutionary process of football (and its training) went on to highlight these three dimensions. However, playing football carried on to be expressed in a mechanistic way, and the separation between the physical, the technical, and the tactical was unquestionable. This reality persisted and solidified the association of football with certain sciences like physiology, biology, and biomechanics, amongst others, whose mechanistic paradigm was evident.

Built on a new stream of scientific thinking, the systematic paradigm - some people agree - sees the game of football as the *interaction* between tactical, technical, physical and psychological dimensions. It tries to create a training methodology that concedes the interaction of the different dimensions into so-called "integrated training". However, as is wont to happen in many revolutions, there is always a certain nostalgia that cannot be overcome; a nostalgia that conditions the step to another level, or to another paradigm.

In the case of "integrated training" there were always two problems that the methodology could never surpass.

The first one comes with the name itself, "integrated training", which suggests a certain "identity crisis". If we consider it "integrated" is it because it is something that can be disintegrated? The questions that subsequently follow are: maybe football can be broken down into tactical, technical, physical and psychological? Maybe football is a whole? Is not Football just a tactical game? In any action, technical ability, run, or manifestation of any kind, is it not a decisional response to a certain situation created by the game? If we understand that it is, the game is tactical, but it will permanently have technical, physical, and psycho-cognitive manifestations. This means, the tactical game *is the whole* and from the moment it gets divided up, it stops being so.

The second problem derives from the persistence of the first one. This means that "integrated training" never managed to liberate itself from the integration and disintegration problem. Even though it tried to promote the interaction between the different dimensions, it permanently suffers from two sub-problems. The first one refers to the control and direction of training; the second, to the lack of contextualization (in other words, the lack of specificity that training shows).

Related to the dimension that assumes the control and direction of training, seen in the first problem, should be the tactical dimension. However, it is the physical dimension that takes that role.

Regarding the lack of context, it is clear that training often fails *the tactical dimension* - the one that controls the process which provokes a non-specificity related to the team. With this we want to say that, even though training may seem specific, because the training situations created belong to the football game, they are not always ideal to bring out the desired behavioural patterns for that team. There is no specificity of team, there is specificity of modality, a generalized specificity and, as a consequence, abstraction.

Aware of these problems, and with a deep understanding of the systemic paradigm, Professor Vítor Frade (first team assistant coach for many seasons at Futebol Clube de Oporto, and simultaneously lecturer at the sport department of Porto University) has, for almost thirty years, developed a football training methodology that finally leaves aside the mechanist paradigm and emphasizes playing as a singular creation and which is, therefore, specific.

He named the operational process that creates play as "Tactical Periodization". "Periodization" because there is a period of time to create the expected game. "Tactical" because the game is decisional, but those decisions, individual or collective, can be different depending on desired behavioural patterns. That is why decisions must not be abstract, but built within the intended behavioural matrix. Decisions must be contextualized and specific to the team.

Thus, the term Tactical Periodization contextualizes the game of a team and creates an identity that directs and orientates all the members of that team, allowing specificity to emerge.

This book, in a simple way, tries to highlight the main foundations of Tactical Periodization. It tries to show the bridges created and used by this methodology, finding support from different knowledge areas. It tries to enhance a different way of looking at the game and training. It can become a turning, or even starting, point towards a different understanding of the training process.

Will this methodology be better or worse than the others? I personally think better. But besides that, one thing I know for sure: this concept of training is nothing more than the search for the essence of Football. It is research into the game as it is, an indivisible game, or, as Vítor Frade says, "An unbreakable game!"

Will somebody who takes this conceptual path be successful? First of all, they must follow the suggested methodological principles, and having done so, success will very much depend on the quality of the playing ideas of the manager. However, the methodology has already brought about a few national championships; from the first team of F.C. Porto, to the greatest exponent of this methodology, José Mourinho, who has already won several national championships in four different countries, Portugal, England, Italy and Spain, several national cups, and the Champions League.

So, Tactical Periodization is a different way of constructing the game, it is, fundamentally, a true operational and philosophical "revolution" of football training.

Guilherme Oliveira, J. (2007)

Introduction

Tactical Periodization is a training methodology that first arose over 30 years ago when Professor Victor Frade, through his experiences, began to question the training methodologies used up to that point.

Understanding that football and team play cannot be understood through classic scientific thought (analytically and decontextualized) - given its wholeness, unpredictability, and nonlinear condition, he decided to search for more suitable theories for the problems of football. Frade arrived at some systemic theories that, together with certain methodological principles, eventually became Tactical Periodization.

Tactical Periodization is a training methodology where the primary concern is the *play* that a team intends to produce in competition. This is why the *playing model* is assumed as a guide for the whole process, using principles, sub-principles and sub-sub-principles to shape it; reaching a certain quality, and specific adaptation, by respecting the methodological principles that sustain it.

This book stems from the need to make this training methodology known outside Portugal.

The purpose of this book is that people who have never heard about Tactical Periodization can understand its foundations, in a simple way. However, the task has not been easy. There have been numerous occasions where we had to undo what was written, and rewrite it because it was too complex.

This task, however, was was much easier thanks to the guidance of Professor Vitor Frade, creator of the methodology itself, and the collaboration of Professor Guilherme Oliveira who helped with his presentations and practical examples.

This book is not meant to be a criticism of other training methodologies, those that have nothing to do with Tactical

Periodization. It is simple vision of a different way of understanding football and its training, a way that the author has had the opportunity to implement and achieve, with this methodology, the desired results.

This book is also a link between the author and a place, a story, a time, people, a thought, a memory, and some feelings…

Chapter 1

Football: A complex phenomenon formed by a system of systems (teams)

"The science of complexity, in living systems, is in charge of the behaviour of the systems in non-linear networks, consisting of a great number of agents where each agent uses some sets of norms, called schemes, to interact with all other agents in the system so they produce a joint action."
Stacey (2001 referenced by Gaiteiro 2006)

The Football Team: an open, adaptive and homeostatic System

"A system is something more (and something less) than the simple sum of its constitutive elements." Moriello (2003)

A system is a "set of elements or parts that interact with each other with the aim of reaching a certain objective." Miriello (2003). Two fundamental features describe the system. The first one is that a change in one part of the system will affect the other parts. The second is the existence of a common goal.

Thus, a football team is a system where a group of players interact with one another to achieve a common goal (a certain way of playing, with the aim of achieving victory – that is the objective of any sport).

When we talk about a system (i.e. a team) we must not forget that it is placed within an environment (context) that will affect both its behaviour and its performance (Moriello 2003). According to Moriello, there are different types of systems, and amongst them we find: "those that present some or much interaction with the environment are named open systems and those that react and adapt to the environment are called adaptive."

A football team, as well as the game (i.e. play) that is produced, is an open and adaptive system due to the high level of interaction with the environment and its adaptive capacity.

Furthermore, a team can also be defined as a "homeostatic" system in the way that "Homeostasis defines the tendency of a system towards dynamic survival. Systems that are highly homeostatic follow the changes of the context through internal structural adjustments," Moriello (2003). This is exactly what happens in a football team, where there is a continuous interchange between internal order and disorder with the aim of structurally adjusting itself depending on the need of the hour.

If a football team is a system, then playing can then be defined as a system of systems – a complex system (Gomes 2006) due to how "it expresses the relations of cooperation between teammates and of opposition with rivals." which is to say the fight between two systems (teams) for a final goal (victory).

Football and the game as a complex phenomenon

"The path pointed out by chaos theory is to address systems (football games) as they are presented, without leaving out any aspect that could help in the true and global vision of the phenomenon being observed. In this aspect it "transcends the boundary lines of knowledge." Andrade (1996 mentioned by Resende 2002)

As per Morin (1999), "Complexity exists when the different components, that constitute a whole, are inseparable and there is an interconnected, interactive tissue between the parts and the whole, and the whole and the parts." The same direction is taken by Vriend (1994 mentioned by Phelan in 2001 and Gaitero in 2006) when he says, "a complex system is a system consisting of a great number of agents that interact between each other in different ways."

Systems, or complex phenomena, besides being characterised by the interconnection and interaction of the different parts, as well as the whole, are also made up of a wide range of uncertainties, chances, etc. that offer even more complexity. Morin (1999) refers to this when he writes, "complexity not only includes quantities of units and interactions that challenge our options for calculation; it also comprehends uncertainties and random phenomena." He adds that, "a phenomenon or complex system has to do with the semi random systems whose order is inseparable from the chances that include them. Complexity is that way linked to a certain mixture of order and disorder," making reference in this last quote to Chaos Theory[1]

Moriello (2003) attributes other characteristics to complex systems. He mentions that their behaviour is often erratic, consisting of a large number of identical elements, and that the "interaction between these elements is local and creates an emerging behaviour that cannot be explained by taking those elements separately." As Capra (1996, mentioned by Gaitero 2006) says, "the whole presents features as a result of the interactions and the relations between its parts and the relation of the whole with the context"; something that makes

---

[1] Chaos theory studies the behaviour of dynamical systems that are highly sensitive to initial conditions—an effect which is popularly referred to as the butterfly effect. Small differences in initial conditions (such as those due to rounding errors in numerical computation) yield widely diverging outcomes for such dynamical systems, rendering long-term prediction impossible in general. (Wikipedia)

it even clearer is the phrase: "The whole is not equal to the sum of its parts," (Morin 2001).

This means that football and the play produced by a team are a complex phenomenon, as they consist of several components (tactical, technical, physical and psychological; and strategic on certain occasions) and moments (offensive moment, defensive moment and its two transitions). They are part of a whole and cannot be seen separately from the rest because these factors are inseparable.

Because football is made up of a number of relatively identical elements (secured by the play of a team) and because of its unpredictability, instability and randomness, "[the] unpredictability and randomness of football make it a multifactor structure of high complexity." Carvalhal (2001)

Garganta also refers to it when he says that, "in the mere appearance of a football game, a very complex phenomena is present, due to the high unpredictability and randomness of the plays." Another feature that frames football within complex phenomena is the existence of the relationship between order and disorder, providing non-linear chaotic phenomena. As Dunning (1994 mentioned by Resende 2002) points out, "the Game (football) is a chaotic event, especially sensitive to the initial conditions. It is one of the most eloquent cases of deterministic chaos, since it is played on the border between chaos and order."

Cunha and Silva (2000 mentioned by Resende 2002) explain this existing relationship between order and disorder in the game when they say that, "the team can be accepted as organized in a deterministic way, but from one manoeuvre to the next one we are shown that the game (football) is organized *catastrophically*."

Summary

A football team is a complex thing. On a basic level, it can be seen as a system that has lots of constituent parts (such as players) that interact with each other, and which strive for a common goal (victory). Interactions between the different parts influence the behaviours of the other parts. Importantly, one should remember that a football team is more than the simple sum of its parts - it is a complex system where the whole (the team) and the parts (such as the players) all affect one another.

Football, as a system, is also influenced by its context. In other words, a football team's functioning and performance is influenced by the environment it operates in, and it adapts its behaviour accordingly. This adaptation sees the team adjusting itself structurally – regularly shifting into an ordered or disordered state – due to the requirements of what is happening on the pitch at any given time.

Looking at things more broadly, when two teams compete on a football field, you have a clash of two systems, so the match (or overall play) becomes a system of systems!

Because there are lots of uncertainties in a football match – people, the weather, the referee, the pitch, the bounce of the ball, etc. – it makes sense to think of the game as a random or semi-random system where you cannot precisely determine or calculate outcomes in advance. Football is a chaotic sport, and the factors that drive it are localised and unpredictable; they cannot be viewed in isolation! They all interact!

When we step back and take a bird's eye view of a football match, we can see that the complex phenomena underpinning football include tactical, technical, physical, psychological and strategic components - as well as 'moments' in the game when play shifts. These moments are a team's attacking and defending phases of play, as well as the transitions between them (e.g. going from attack to defence, and going from defence to attack). The whole point of Tactical Periodization is that these moments are a 'whole' — they cannot be viewed in isolation from each other.

Chapter 2

Systemic Thinking: a new way of dealing with the world. "Tactical Periodization": a new way of dealing with football.

"Unfortunately, we have followed the model of Descartes (contemporary to Pascal) who praised the division of the reality of problems. However, a whole produces qualities that are not present in the individual parts. The whole is never just the sum of the parts. It is something more." Edgar Morin (1984)

The emergence of new thinking (complex or systemic thinking)

"Complex thinking is the one that, assuming its uncertainty, is capable of conceiving the organization. Its role consists in gathering, contextualizing, globalizing, and at the same time, being able to recognize the singular, the individual, the specific." Gaiteiro (2006)

As per Gomes (in 2006 mentioning Durand, 1979), "Western science was oriented and built on the contributions of classic rationalism, inherited from Aristotle and developed by Descartes." Classic scientific thinking took the command of the intellect as the world reference. It was taken as the unquestionable 'one and only truth' overshadowing all other philosophies.

However, as per Capra (2007), in the West the "scientific tradition is based on linear thinking," although systems are nonlinear. That is why classic scientific thinking is based on a causal and mechanistic vision, making it weak as a structure when explaining the great problems of living systems. It is settled on analytic, divisive, and broken-up thought - the fragmentation of the parts of a system implies not only the separation of parts, but also the annulment of their properties. Another characteristic that defines this thinking is that it considers its truth to be absolute.

However, the need for a new thinking arises - a new way of seeing the world. As Capra (1996 referenced by Gaiteiro 2006) explained, "The main problems of our time cannot be understood in isolation... systemic problems require a radical change in our perceptions, thoughts and values."

That is how a new intellectual paradigm arose, supported by authors such as Von Bertalanffy, Edgar Morin, and Le Moigne. Contrary to classical scientific thinking, going from the existing mechanistic vision to a vision that is focused on the whole, "These latest theories are known as systemic theories, and their implied way of thinking is known as systemic thinking." Capra (1996 mentioned by Gaiteiro 2006).

Systemic thinking is mainly based on the concept that "the whole is not equal to the sum of the parts," Morin (2001). In turn, Capra (1996 referenced by Gaiteiro 2006) wrote, "The whole presents features as a result of the interactions and relations between their parts and the relation of the whole and its context."

Capra questioned the classical scientific method by asserting, "These features are destroyed when the system is divided, physically or theoretically, into isolated elements." In other words, things must always be contextualized. Gaiteiro (2006) made the point clearly, "Understanding things systemically means, literally, placing them within a context, establishing the nature of their relations."

Another essential feature that defines systemic thinking, also brought up by Gaiteiro (2006), is in understanding that "objects are, first of all, immersed in networks of relationships, and these are also related to other networks." Accordingly, we can come to the conclusion that there are no 'parts', but instead there is a huge network that hosts a multitude of interconnected networks. Hence 'separation' is incoherent. The last great characteristic shows that inside a system there are other systems, with the same or different degrees of complexity.

The need for a systemic vision for that complex phenomenon called football

"Tactical Periodization addresses the complex phenomena, as it contemplates the object in its entirety and context." Gaiteiro (2006)

Cartesian thinking - analytic and divisive - also reached football and team play. Its intention was to simplify the inherent complexity of play, fragmenting the parts, decontextualizing the different dimensions, isolating factors and parts (tactical, technical, physical and psychological), as well as the moments that form them (offensive, defensive and the transitions, attack-defence and defence-attack), without observing the principle of an "unbreakable entirety" that comes within the game.

The eagerness of classic scientific knowledge to measure things skewed our knowledge, isolating its aspects and moments; things now worked in an isolated and analytical way, and so in a decontextualized way.

In response to this, Morin (1985) wrote, "It is still difficult to understand that the dysfunction and fragmentation of knowledge affects not only the possibility of an understanding of the knowledge but also our possibilities of knowing about ourselves and about the world, provoking what Gusdorf rightly calls 'the pathology of knowledge'."

This 'pathology of knowledge' affected football through conventional periodization (the theory created by Matveiev), which fragmented football into its four factors and moments, isolating and decontextualizing them. It still rules today. To Frade (2003 referenced by Gaiteiro 2006), "Most people have not yet managed to remove from their heads the biggest conceptual cancer: the phases, periods, stages, loads." He was referring, in this way, to Matveiev's theoretical features.

However, there are many authors and football professionals who choose another way, and a different vision (systemic thinking). It is thinking that defends a totality; thinking that integrates all the game's dimensions and moments.

José Mourinho took the same direction when he wrote for the Única magazine of the Expresso newspaper (Amieiro, Oliveira, Resende and Barreto, 2006): "I defend the sum of the work, not separating the physical, technical, tactical and psychological components…"

He also referred to the wholeness, in this case the one formed by the moments of the game (Amieiro 2005) when he wrote, "I cannot decide what is most important, to defend well or to attack well, because I cannot manage detaching these two moments. I think of the team as a whole and its work also as a whole."

We also see the need for non-reductionist thinking, that understands the real problems that affect complex phenomena and, in our special case, football. We need a new vision that, as stated by Morin (1990), changes "the paradigm of disjunction/reduction/one dimensionality for a paradigm of distinction/conjunction that allows distinguishing without disjoining, associating without identifying or reducing."

We are talking about passing from the existing methodology (i.e. reductionist, isolating, analytic) to a methodology that understands the entirety of the factors and moments that form football, *without separating them during training.*

The emergence of Tactical Periodization (which clearly sets itself apart from "integrated training")

"In Tactical Periodization this order of dividing the object does not exist. More than a 'theory of divisions' it is a 'theory of synergies', it is the articulation of its components, that brings complexity, enrichment, but above all feasibility, because it is coherent and specific to the object that it transforms." Gaiteiro (2006)

By acknowledging, in chapter 1, that football is a complex system of systems (complex phenomena), we create the need for new thinking, which understands that the knowledge of the parts depends on the knowledge of the whole, and that the knowledge of the whole depends on the knowledge of the parts. That is how Tactical Periodization was born. Subsequently, our understanding (i.e. our understanding of what Tactical Periodization is) leads to a training methodology that respects the whole (principle of "unbreakable entirety") of the game.

It also recognizes the "principle of incompleteness and uncertainty" (Morin 1990), as well as the alternation between order and disorder that, as mentioned in the previous chapter, relates to chaos theory (complex systems). This thinking then leads to a "non-reductionist knowledge." based on the "acknowledgment of the unfinished and incompleteness of all knowledge." In other words, a methodology emerges separating us from the factors and moments that form the game, and at the same time recognising the uncertainty that the game brings with it.

However, even though Tactical Periodization is based on the whole, it does not ignore the individual. As per Morin (1982 referencing Pascal, mentioned by Gomes in 2006), it is impossible "to know the parts without knowing the whole as

23

much as it is to know the whole without knowing the parts." This, therefore, moves us away from holistic thinking (i.e. "integrated training") as it "neglects the dynamic role of its parts, of the interconnected interactions of all the parts of the team, of individual characteristics and the relationships between the players in the different moments of the game" Gomes (2006). In other words, integrated training is abstract.

Even though integrated training includes all the components of the game, it treats them in a specific way, and does not look to the series of interconnections (existing between the different parts) in a singular and specific way.

To Morin, Tactical Periodization is "apt to connect; contextualize and include, but at the same time to recognize the singular, the individual and the specific."

So what are we saying? We are saying that Tactical Periodization gives more importance to its collective aspect. As per Frade (1985), "The 'whole' is way more than the sum of the 'parts' in the organization of a complex system." But we must not forget singular and specific, giving them the importance that they deserve.

Tactical Periodization is, then, a training process that emphasizes the organizational aspect of the team, working the game model in the way that the coach wants to achieve; focusing on players in an individual way that is appropriate to their specific 'play'. A winger, for example, in a defensive, offensive or transitional specific drill, will be working individually, developing the 'play' he will have to do as a winger. But, at the same time, he will be part of a collective organization. This is why Tactical Periodization does not allow "the team to get reduced to an analysis of its players in individual terms." Gomes (2006). Morin (1997 referenced by the same author in 2006) expressed it differently: "The global identity is superior to the sum of its parts."

So, Tactical Periodization looks for a new paradigm that carries, as per Morin "the principle of a multiplex unit, escaping over (holism), and below (reductionism) the abstract unit." That is what Descombes (referenced in Kaufmann and Quéré, 2001 mentioned by Gomes in 2006) calls a "pseudo-holistic" conception. In other words, a collective concept that does not revoke individuality (Gomes 2006). As the author wrote (in 2006 mentioning Cunha and Silva, 1999), "The relations and interactions between players are the ones turning the game into a collective activity."

Summary

This chapter has looked at how football, and training in particular, has (historically) been subject to a scientific method that breaks things apart into their constituent components. A scientific method that reduces the whole, and which looks at components and topics *in isolation*.

Systemic thinking, on the other hand, is based on the concept that "the whole is *not equal* to the sum of its parts". Thinking about complex phenomena (such as football) from a 'systemic' perspective means placing everything within a context. It means you need to establish and understand the nature of the constituent parts of the system *and* their interconnected relationships with other parts of the system!

Systemic thinking suggests that breaking football down into isolated phases, periods, and actions (amongst other things) is *not* the most effective way forward because that is *not* how football is played. We need to think about football – and how to train players – in a way that integrates all the actual game's dimensions and moments. Mourinho's quote is key here: "I defend the totality of the work, not separating the physical, technical, tactical and psychological components…"

Since a competitive match involves all of football's elements coming together at the same time, training must replicate this complexity. There is no point in getting a player to carry out the same action (during practice) if it bears little relevance to how such an action would take place in a game. Training must look to replicate match situations. Old skill drills, such as players lining up to do a one-two with a coach before taking a shot against a set 'keeper' from 20 yards are abstracted moments of the game. Do you, as a coach, feel such an artificial scenario might actually happen on match day?

Training must represent the totality of the game. Tactical Periodization does not allow "the team to get reduced to an analysis of its players in individual terms." It focuses on what the 'team' is seeking to do at all times and how individual players contribute to the overall game plan (and style) in *all* ways (physical, technical, tactical and psychological) at all times.

Chapter 3

The playing model as a guide to the whole process

"A theory (Playing Model) is not the knowledge; it allows the knowledge. A theory is not an arrival; it is the possibility of a departure. A theory is not a solution; it is the possibility of dealing with a problem." Morin

Football: A phenomenon that is constructed and deterministic (it is never finished)

"Playing is an outcome constructed by the process of training, towards a future that we want to reach." Frade (2004 mentioned by Gomes 2006)

The football that a team produces is not a natural phenomenon, but the result of a constructed phenomenon. Besides being a constructed phenomenon, we can also say that the game of football is deterministic in the sense that - at the time of the construction - we know what we want to build, and what we want to reach in the future.

Accordingly, we can see that there are different types of football, because every coach has their own style. In turn, context provides uniqueness and, as we know, no context is equal to another context.

However, we must be aware of the unpredictability of the future, which will force us to reshape our early ideas, making football an entity that is always under construction, by the coach and by the player… adapting itself to different situations. That is why we can never consider football 'a completed job'.

So the thinking behind the game of football (the thinking done by coaches) and elaborated upon (through the training process) needs to be seen as a constructed and deterministic phenomenon; always under construction, modifying and reshaping certain aspects of the initial idea, without the need to change its background.

We must not make the mistake of thinking that we are modifying the initial idea of the game (that is not what we are talking about). What we modify are certain aspects that surround our idea of the game – these changing aspects ensure the game is always incomplete.

Imagine that you get hired as a coach by a club. You arrive with your idea of the game (conditioned by the football you have seen and experienced) and you then try to make it real, conveying it to your players, through training, so they understand it and put it into practice during games. Your idea of the game in the attacking phase, for example, is to arrive in the opposition's half with organized attacks by the wings, with short passes. So, you train to produce this style of play during the first two months. However, you then realize you have a striker with certain qualities, who likes to make contact with crossed balls and then position the ball sideways towards a teammate. As such, you modify the way your team plays the ball after a recovery, playing long balls looking for this striker to then play to the sides. We can see that you have modified certain aspects of your game, but that does not mean you have lost your identity. This modification process is never finished, but change does not mean having to stop playing the type of football that the coach had in mind from the beginning.

The coach as constructor of a determined football

"...success in football has a thousand recipes. The coach must believe in one, and seduce the players with it." Valdano (1998 mentioned by Gomes 2006)

The coach is mainly responsible for the construction of the football that we are trying to achieve. The coach will intervene directly in the management of the training process. He is the thinker and the leader of the team.

The coach must have a clear idea of the game (Tactical Culture[2]), this idea must be singular and specific and it will be determined by his own football history and by the type of football that he has seen and loved.

However, the coach cannot limit himself only to thinking about the game. He must also transmit his thinking through the process of training. He will have to do it in a brief and clear manner, in such a way that his players understand clearly what he is looking for.

To achieve this goal through the training process, Frade (2005) has suggested, "the coach must be educated as a reflexive person, organized, thoughtful, to whom every certainty is uncertain. The coach will not do something just because he once saw it being done, but because his intuition and reflection will show him the best way to achieve the intended goal." Frade is making clear that the coach must not blindly copy the work and drills of others, instead he must generate them, through a unique and singular process (developed by him), concordant with the context around him, and reflective of his own work.

---

[2] Way of seeing and understanding Football. It is the football that the coach has in mind.

Frade also explains, "the coach will be conscious that the periodization that leads to a certain way of playing is a long process." This means that to create a team, with its own identity, the path is long; he goes further when stating that this process must be thought from: "formation through to Superior Performance."[3]

The playing model: the football we want to achieve

"The most important thing in a team is to have a certain model, certain principles, to know them well, to interpret them well, regardless of whether they are used by this or that player." Mourinho (2002 mentioned by Amieiro 2005).

The playing model in football is normally misunderstood. Most of the time, people refer to it as the system or scheme of play used; the initial system/formation that the team presents on the playing field.

But the playing model is more than that. As Portolés (2007) says, "A playing model is something that identifies a certain team. It is not only a playing system, it is not only the positioning of the players, it is how those players interact with each other and how they express their way of seeing football." In other words, it is the organization that a team presents for each moment of play, on a regular basis. To Amieiro (2005): "The identity of a team is nothing more than maintaining regularly the organization it aims for."

---

[3] We talk about Superior Performance, differentiating it from High Performance "in the way that the objective comes from the conscious determination of achieving the maximum in all competitions." Gaiteiro (2006). This means, all teams whose actual objective is to win all competitions.

30

We could say that the playing model is a future vision of what we want the team to achieve, on a regular basis, during the different moments of the game. It is the game that the coach would like the team to play, just as Carvalhal (2001) says, "[the playing model] is the future, what we want to achieve and what I am constantly visualizing, it is what I want, it is where I want to get to even knowing that I will never get there… It is the idea of play that gives me the coordinates to work, to guide and to achieve the maximum level of play."

The playing model therefore implies knowing well what we want to achieve during each moment of the game. As such, we need to define a series of behaviours (Principles[4], Subprinciples[5]), as well as links between them; they will allow us to have a playing identity. This is what Carvalhal (2001) means when he says, "The playing model depends on a system of relations that articulate a way of playing, not just any way of playing. A way based on a specific structure." For Oliveira, Resende, and Barreto R (2006), "The playing model is, in truth, a complex of collective and individual references, and those references are the playing principles conceived by the coach."

These principles and subprinciples must be clearly defined and explained to the players that form the team in a way that all of them understand what the coach wants, since, as Oliveira (2003) states, "the playing model is essentially mental, because the players are the ones playing and the players have interpretations and those interpretations, when they start

---

4 Principles are general game behaviours created by the Coach. "The principle is the beginning of a behaviour that the coach wants the team, in collective terms, and the players, in individual terms, to acquire." (Oliveira mentioned by Gomes 2006)

5 Sub Principles are more specific behaviours of play.

interacting with each other, most of the time are independent." But, achieving this is not an easy task and, as mentioned earlier, takes time. Achieving this will be "determined by the capacity-quality of a player and also, on a larger scale, by how the coach is capable of unifying the individuals into something superior, into a team." (Portolés 2007).

Therefore, the more elaborate a playing model is and the better explained it is to the players, the clearer it will be for the players to know what to do during certain moments of the game, without making it mechanistic, because our process (Tactical Periodization) promotes a "non-mechanistic process"[6].

Contrary to what many people think, the playing model cannot be rigid. It must be flexible depending on the context, it also must be malleable, and able to be modified depending on the requirements at a certain moment.

In an interview on June 6, 2003, to the F.C. Barcelona website, Jaume Llauradó (then candidate for the presidency of Barcelona) said that one of the main challenges of the Sporting Department will be to "define a playing model, a specific style, the will remain beyond the coaches and players over time." While it is true that a Club must have a football history, we must not fall into the rigid thinking of playing one way (although we must have an initial idea, it will vary its shape), because, as mentioned earlier, each context will be different).

In response to this, Frade (2003) highlights that, "the playing model is never complete because the process, as it happens, will create signs that will be interpreted by the coach, who will make adjustments to stimulate a higher quality. Hence the existence of not only one developed playing model but several

---

[6] See Chapter 6

developed playing models." Also, Castelo (1994) says, "as a playing model is being built, it is necessary to question it systematically, meaning that we construct it progressively, before deconstructing it and reconstructing it." To do this, Frade (1985) adds, the playing model must be always analysed and questioned: "The Playing Model, as a final goal, must be constantly visualized, this means, maintaining the future as a causal element of the behaviour."

Another feature to be highlighted and one that assumes fundamental importance to the whole process, is that the playing model must allow creativity[7] by the player. Freitas (2004): "The playing model will be richer if it allows, as much as possible, players to expand their own creativity and talent in the game, without impacting upon the premises of each model."

This way we can say that the playing model is a set of behaviours, which the coach aims to manifest in a regular and systematic way, in the four recognized moments of the Game (offensive organization, defensive organization and then two transitional phases from one organization to the other one). These behaviours are reproduced as principles, subprinciples and subprinciples of the subprinciples (also known as sub subprinciples). When these behaviours are articulated between each other, they generate a certain way of playing, the so-called DNA of the Team. Furthermore, the playing model must improve day by day, and allow for the creativity of players, and the peculiarities of the circumstances. Frade (2007) states that "The model is everything! It must be understood that the model represents intention (i.e. the intention of the coach to play a certain way) developed and made tangible in all moments, from planning to fulfilment to the consideration of what happened (taking into account what we want)."

---

[7] See Chapter 6.

That is why a Playing Model cannot be adopted. It must be created. When you model and operate a system, things that were unknown to the coach will happen, and will subsequently become part of the Model, leading to the "subprinciples that are the exact result of the here and now." Frade (2007).

The importance of the playing model in the training process (modelling)

"The preoccupation is, from the first day, to get the team to play like the coach wants, according to a Playing Model." Frade (1985 mentioned by Freitas 2004)

To Le Moigne (mentioned by Garganta 1996) "the understanding of the complex system supposes its modeling, this modeling must be understood as the action of intentional collaboration and construction, by composing symbols, models susceptible of making a complex phenomenon into something comprehensible."

So, under the systemic point of view of Tactical Periodization - in its search to reduce the complexity of football's complex phenomena, to achieve high performance - there must be a modelling of the particular game that we are trying to achieve.

To Frade (2007) "the model is essential because, as I understand training, training corresponds to learning and in this case, learning a way of playing that has to become customary, a way of playing that implies starting from the most essential or fundamental aspects (most structural) of the game." This will be achieved through the division of the principles and subprinciples that form our game, which will then configure the playing model, that will provide an identity to our team and which will guide the whole training process. A training process that will respect the principle of the "unbreakable entirety" of the game, managing to "reduce without impoverishing"[8], in order to simplify things.

For Frade (2007), the coach that practices Tactical Periodization must be guided by the playing model, and follow the methodological principles that support it. "Modelling allows for the development of characteristics (the identity) of the team through its consistencies or patterns – organization. And to develop that model – or better, that modelling – certain methodological principles must be considered, taking into account human limitations and the fundamental need to achieve a quality adjustment through such modelling.

This way we can see that a training methodology must be based on the play that the coach wants. In other words, it must be based on the playing model, as Le Moigne says, "Models are inevitable elements in the construction of reality and, at the same time, they provide informative tools to construct it." Frade (2007) adds, "(Tactical Periodization) is only a model when there is modelling, this is when the process is tangible (developed). For this, there is the "operationalization" of play (the model concept) which only happens when there is specificity."

With training, as laid out by Oliveira (1991), "The Playing Model comes as a guide to the whole phenomena, and is the one that defines and points to how the different components must be treated."

---

[8] Performing drills that simplify the game without losing its essence.

Creating a "mental landscape" of the playing model in the heads of the players

"A mental landscape must be created because the development of a game must be born in the head of the players first." Frade (2003 mentioned by Martins 2003)

According to Damásio (2003 mentioned by Freitas 2004) "The perception of objects and situations, inside of the organism (imaginings), or on the outside (images coming from spatial sensors), requires images." In that case, it is extremely important to train in contexts that are similar to the ones we will face during the match. To Freitas (2004) "The coach must then use spaces according to his playing model so the players have a correct perception of the space reference inherent to their way of playing." In other words, every situation must be practiced in the area or areas of the field where we want them to happen, provoking the images that Damásio was talking about.

Another important aspect is to present to the players, in a visual way, the playing model, itself, creating an image of it in their heads, Oliveira (2003 mentioned by Freitas, S. in 2004) affirms, "With the visual presentation of the playing model, the coach and the player have a precise reference to help with the fine-tuning of the action." That way, the individual understanding of each player is as similar as possible to his team mates, achieving the common logic aimed for. For Frade (2003 mentioned by Martins in 2003, Gomes 2006) "a mental landscape must be created because the development of the game must be born first in the head of the players." As Gomes (2006) adds, "This aspect is crucial for the decisions and interactions of the players to be anticipated by teammates according to a group of guidelines for each moment of the game."

Also, to visualize the playing model, it also helps if we understand the complete game that we want to create, so we can later, with simplified or reduced manoeuvres, understand the parts in a contextualized way (more detail in Chapter 11).

Another way of achieving a collective understanding will be, once the players clearly know their identity and their role in the team, to change their positions during training, so they also understand perfectly this collective/complete game from the perspective of their teammates. It is about changing, for example, the position of a striker with a winger and vice versa, so these players can have a better understanding of the behaviours of their teammates in certain situations. But for this, as mentioned earlier, they must know to perfection their part in the game in relation to the broader collective game.

Summary

The playing model is the idealised form of football that we want to achieve. The model is the considered intention of the coach to play in a particular way. Systems, formations, organisational structure, players, plus other factors will all help to configure the playing model. It is the headline concept and it covers what we want to accomplish during all moments of the game. The plan can be broken down into principles, sub-principles and more – which all interact with each other.

The playing model cannot be completely rigid. There must be a certain adaptability based on the requirements of any given moment.

A playing model is the starting point for creating a team, and the team's way of playing is converted from this model onto the pitch through training. In other words, play is a constructed phenomenon that originates in the mind of the coach. Every coach has his own model, based on where he finds himself at any time (i.e. there is a context). No two contexts are the same, so no model can just be adopted from someone else willy nilly. Models must be generated.

Importantly, the playing model is never a 'done deal'; it is always evolving – being modified by the resources at your disposal, the skills of the players you work with, the challenges you face, your own self-reflection and analysis, and more. The playing model is never complete because it is always being deconstructed, reconstructed, and improved. Your playing model must allow players to be creative, the model will become richer for it.

As the coach, you are the 'thinker and leader of the team'. You must have a clear idea of the game and what you want; your clear idea is typically influenced by all your preceding experiences of the game. Training is how you transmit your thinking to your players. They need to understand what you are looking to achieve.

The playing model and the way you want your team to play needs to be modelled on the pitch, and this occurs during training. Training will focus on the principles and sub principles of the game to build 'the whole'; we must never forget the game is an unbreakable entirety – you cannot treat elements in isolation; they must conform to the big picture.

The modelling that your team does during training must be based on how the game is actually played (realism, please) and specifically how you (as the coach) want the game to be played. It is *your* model. For the playing model to become real, it must be performed and practiced as closely to match conditions as possible.

Your playing model must be absorbed by players as a 'mental landscape'; they must be able to unambiguously visualise what you are trying to achieve. The decisions and interactions of players need to be anticipated by teammates according to a group of guidelines for each moment of the game. Each player needs to know exactly what his colleagues are likely to do, at any time.

As coach, change your players' positions during training, so they understand perfectly what you are seeking to accomplish both from their own perspective and the perspective of their teammates. For example, change the position of a striker with a winger and vice versa; in doing so these players will understand better the behaviours of their teammates in certain situations. Every situation must be practiced in the area or areas of the pitch where we want them to happen. This will cement the images we want our players to recognise and subsequently act upon.

Chapter 4

The tactical supradimension to achieve the intended game

"Football is a modality with very specific features, therefore preparation and training will have to be determined by a specific orientation. Taking into account that there are different types of football with different characteristics, these will impact on the specific attitudes that players have at a tactical–technical level and, as a consequence, in the other components." Resende (2002)

As mentioned, Tactical Periodization respects the principle of an "unbreakable entirety of the game." so that each drill addresses the four dimensions that form football, as well as its four moments, being the principles and subprinciples of the game. Thus, training is the mechanism that enables players to conceive the way of playing that the coach expects to achieve.

However, despite the generalization of the practice, the four dimensions that create football must be organized according to the practice in question. If the playing model guides the whole process, then the tactical aspect/dimension will always guide the entire practice, and the other elements will appear as a consequence of this.

As Frade (2003 mentioned by Freitas in 2004) points out, "The tactical is not physical, nor technical, nor psychological, but it needs all of them to happen." Furthermore, "Let's understand that any technical or physical action always has an underlying tactical intention." Amieiro, Oliveira, Resende, & Barreto (2006)

Therefore, the tactical aspect appears as a Supradimension that guides the whole training process. Oliveira understands it in the same way when he says, "the implemented[9] Playing Model and its respective principles must be subject to a careful process of periodization and also to dynamic approaches; so that the physical, technical and psychological components are driven by the tactical component but always in parallel."

In other words, tactical training is extremely important, focusing on all the aspects that the coach wants (playing model) on the field, and across the different moments that football has (offensive, defensive, transition attack-defense and transition defense-attack). Hence, it is vital for the coach to have a tactical culture clearly defined for each moment of the game and, based on it, to follow a coherent process (operationalization of this game concept).

Complexity simplified through the disintegration of the principles and sub-principles (that form the Playing Model)

"The big game principle is constituted of a group of sub-principles, of sub-principles of the sub-principles, and sub-sub-sub-principles that refer to the more particularized relations between the players and the materialization of that principle." Gomes (2006)

To tactically periodize is, as we have mentioned, to guide the training process so that players acquire the principles and sub-principles of the game desired by the Coach. These form the basis of training, with the objective of achieving the desired playing model. It is not about performing games in a way as specific as possible, because we will not reduce complexity in

---

[9] The author does not use this term since the Playing Model is created by the Coach, not adopted.

this way, but it is about elaborating manoeuvres that simplify the understanding of the football we want to achieve. In order to do this we have to break apart, or disintegrate, the principles and sub-principles of the game.

The principles are general behaviors that the coach wants to achieve in his game. To Oliveira (mentioned by Gomes, M. in 2006) "the principle is the beginning of a behaviour that a coach wants the team to assume, in collective terms, and the players in individual ones." In other words, it would never be an aim by itself. For instance, a coach wants, when the team wins possession of the ball, to play long passes looking for the head of the striker, so he can deflect the ball towards one of the wingers. This would be a principle of the game. However, what happens next is not determined. The striker can orientate the ball to one side or the other, or he can, depending on his perspective, control the ball and wait for his teammates to support him. Or he can pass with one touch to the teammate facing him. Accordingly, we can see that the team has a principle to achieve, without it restricting the team. Also, a "principle is conditioned by the characteristics of the players… With this, we can say that the principles, recreated by the players and the team, must lead to a creative rise in the quality of the game." Gomes (2006).

Subprinciples are more specific behaviours that happen within the general behaviour.

It is through the principles and subprinciples, as well as their articulation that we can create an "order in the development of the game, turning it into something deterministic; this means that it turns the incalculable predictability of the events into potential predictability," Frade (1998 mentioned by Gomes in 2006), showing a defined game identity… its DNA.

Tactical Periodization allows for the fragmentation of principles and subprinciples, and the connections that exist between them, without the need to isolate the different components and moments that create the game. This is because, in each principle of the game, there is a presence of the whole game. In other words, it allows for the "reduction without weakening" approach we have been talking about, creating exercises in more reduced spaces and with fewer players, simplifying the complexity of the game without separating it from the "whole." This approach respects the principle of an "unbreakable entirety" to the game.

So, the exercises must be a simplification of the game, of complex structures, through the principles and subprinciples, which conform to the playing model. As an example, we will take the defensive principle of pressure. We want our team to create high pressure during the match, however, we are not achieving this, because the players have not understood properly when we have to do so. Thus, we decide to work on the subprinciple of pressure in the offensive sector; namely we work with the three attackers as to how they must press and when. Once this concept is clear and they start doing it properly (this may take 10 minutes, 10 days, or even 10 months) we can then add the middle sector, connecting one subprinciple with the other. Once this is achieved, we will then be able to connect it together with the subprinciple of pressure in the defensive sector, achieving the principle at a general level.

If this training methodology is based on the operationalization of the playing model, created by the coach, and the corresponding principles and subprinciples that shape it, then the concern will to be, from the first day, how to make the team play as the coach wants. This, as per the playing model, is the tactical factor that drives the other factors. As such, there is specificity in all aspects, linked to a specific way of playing.

In reference to this, Carvalhal (2001) wrote that his "team is organized to play from day one and at the same time, modeled to all levels: physical, technical, tactical and psychological. We pay attention to all factors." He added,

"The physical aspect is very important but the coordination of all the physical, technical and psychological work comes from the tactical work."

To Portolés (2007), training must be guided by the tactical aspect, with the playing model a priority because, "every coach must prioritize when planning training." These priorities "must be a reference to what he wants his team to do, which identity he wants his team to have… Everything you do will be determined or guided by the playing model that you want in place." He also warns that it must happen from the first day of training "because that is what leaves a mark." In reference to that, he recalled how, during his time at Albacete fifteen years ago, "Our success was that we had a very well-defined playing model and it was not common to find teams with such a developed model." Also Schuster (2007) highlighted the importance of working the tactical aspect at all times, when in an interview for a sports newspaper he said: "positioning is not invented nor improvised, we are practicing it all the time."

With Jose Mourinho, the playing model is a priority: "One of the premises of my work is that the players, from a tactical point of view, know exactly how we play, what we play for, what the roles are for of each of them," something achieved through training and understanding the different principles and subprinciples without losing sight of the "whole" (as we will see in Chapter 11).

All of them agree that achieving a playing model takes time, so a coach must practise it from day one, subordinating everything to the tactical supradimension.

Specificity: principle of principles

"The principle of specificity will manage Tactical Periodization" Frade (2001 mentioned by Tavares, 2003)

The fact that the tactical supradimension must orientate each exercise, creating a certain way of playing, characterized by certain principles and subprinciples that form a playing model gives a certain specificity to each exercise. In other words, we are always training our game and this makes the training specific to our way of playing.

We are talking about a total specificity in each of the dimensions; in other words, a specificity that accompanies the game and that the team is trying to develop in all its factors (tactical, technical, physical and psychological specificity).

This is how, in our methodology, the principle of specificity appears, and it must be accomplished during each moment of training, becoming the 'principle of principles' with Tactical Periodization.

"It is not enough to agree that it is important, it is a must that this principle becomes the Principle of Principles, the bastion of the whole implemented methodology" (Oliveira (1991) mentioned by Freitas in 2004). Specificity steers Tactical Periodization.

Nevertheless, we must distinguish between overall and dimensional specificities. As Oliveira (1991 mentioned by Freitas,in 2004) explained: "we can only call [overall] specificity if there is a permanent and constant relation between the psycho-cognitive, tactic-technical, physical and coordinative components in permanent correlation with the implemented playing model and its respective principles."

So, specificity in playing carries a physical, technical and psychological (dimensional) specificity. As the author says, "all activity must be always orientated by the specific effort required by the playing model." Faria (1999 mentioned by Freitas 2004) refers to this when he explained: "it is not enough with a specificity-modality, a sub-specificity-playing model is necessary," displaying the existing difference between "Integrated Training and Tactical Periodization."

Resende (2002) explains the difference between specificities when he affirms, "Specific training is different to training consisting of situational exercises. It's important to highlight that specificity needs to be worked in an effective way so that the loads that the players are subject to are interconnected to the implemented playing model and its respective principles. Otherwise we are simply talking about situational exercises."

Rui Faria (mentioned by Carvalhal 2001) refers to this when he stated, "Tactical Periodization/Systemic Modeling forces a breakdown of the game/complexity, articulating it into complex actions, and behavioural actions of a certain way of playing. This articulation emerges depending on what we are trying to achieve – a concept of intentional actions, a game culture – and as a consequence, a specific adaptation that is tactical/systemic (understood as a culture), bringing with it technical, physical and psychological aspects. This concept underscores the principle of specificity." The same author made clear, "…adaptations are not limited only to physiological changes but also, as per Bompa (1983), to precise implications in the technical, tactical and psychological factors."

We can then say that Tactical Periodization, based on this specificity, works such that the attack, the defence and the different transitions, interact with no established order (i.e. no part is more important than another part). Training is therefore akin to simulation, they should be as real as possible to the games we want to play! As Le Moigne (mentioned by Gutiérrez 2002) says, "It requires an analogy of simulated behaviours, simulations accomplished over symbolic models. And the simulation is not neutral: it affects the models itself… All knowledge is structurally circular and self-referential. The effective use of a model requires the previous acknowledgement of its necessary ambiguity."

This way, training that ensures the organization of a team must simulate moments of competitive play, and this simulation must be converted into exercises that are in context with a competitive reality. "We can say that two subjects, with identical structural foundations, can differ drastically in their performance and efficacy on the behaviours, depending on their capacity to activate and direct, in a controlled and precise way, such behaviours towards the desired final aim." Portolés (2007). Furthermore, "This personal capacity of activation and controlled direction is a complex function itself but even more so when the goal to be achieved has not been perfectly defined from the beginning."

That is why we must achieve the largest number of players thinking the same way in a certain situation. They must have a clear aim (principles and subprinciples of the game and the playing model) from day one. This is achieved through exercises that simulate the reality of the game we want to achieve.

Tactical Periodization always works through specificity, leaving no room for certain analytics or out of context exercises. That is why it rejects isolated physical or technical exercises that do not relate to the playing model, as this leads to lack of specificity in the process.

"Integrated" Training must not be confused with Tactical Periodization. We are talking about a specificity connected to the way of playing, different from the playing specificity that prevails in the "integrated" way (although obviously it also has specific exercises).

Summary

Tactical Periodization respects the principle of an "unbreakable entirety of the game." so that *each* drill addresses *each* of the four dimensions. One dimension, however, should be considered the 'Daddy-o' or Supradimension and that is the tactical dimension. Everything else – physical, technical, psychological - should stem from your tactical thinking which comes from your playing model.

The tactical supradimension guides the whole training process. A coach needs to know *exactly* what he wants his team to do, tactically, for each moment and transition of the game.

The coach's overall view of how he wants the game to be played – the playing model - can be thought of as the top level principle, which is made up of progressively more granular/explicit principles and sub-principles beneath it. So, the playing model might be "fast-flowing, on-the-floor, attacking football through the thirds"; this is then made up of specific sub principles (and sub sub principles) that dictate *how* this principle is actually accomplished – related to specific positions, players, moments of the game. There can be a large number of principles, sub principles and sub sub principles.

These principles and sub-principles form the basis of training. It is worth noting that some principles and sub-principles will be governed or constrained by the features of the players that the coach has at his or her disposal. You cannot play a dribbling-based game if none of your players can dribble.

A principle need not limit a team. The example in the chapter highlighted how a long ball towards a striker can lead to different subsequent patterns and plays. By having principles and sub principles – the players and team know what they need to do which means that greater predictability can be brought to events.

Subprinciples (such as defending in different thirds, as per the example above) should be connected to one another, as appropriate, to form a higher level principle.

Training should *always* be focused on achieving the desired playing model. Training drills should look to simplify the complexity of the game of football so that players understand what to do across scenarios.

Coaches recommend that training operates – *from day one* – on seeking to accomplish the playing model. To reiterate the above: "the physical aspect is very important but the coordination of all the physical, technical and psychological work comes from the tactical work."

Training needs to be specific to the demands of the game of football. This means you should not have training sessions that are more appropriate for other disciplines (and not particularly applicable to football). Whilst it might be fun to have players go to the boxing gym – how does thwacking a punchbag benefit football? When coming up with a training plan for the year, you need to focus, first and foremost, on the elements that you want your team to develop on the pitch; it is these training drills and exercises that develop the four moments of the game.

Training needs to be specifically related to what the playing model seeks to accomplish and its principles and sub-principles. The coach should have specific aims of what he wants the team to do. Training is ostensibly simulation; it should be as closely related to match play as possible. If it is not related to match play, it is not specific.

The headline aim of training is all about tactics, tactics, tactics – the other dimensions develop based on the tactical vision of the playing model. Tactical, physical, technical and psychology elements are not developed independently. Under Tactical Periodization, you train the whole and it is unbreakable. Every training exercise or drill should focus on a moment of the game (e.g. transition from attack to defence, or offensive organisation) and the tactics the coach wants his team to produce. It is highly important to note that training 'simulation' feeds back into the playing model and affects it. This feedback loop should be embraced.

Specificity basically means exercises must relate to competitive reality and training must adhere to this principle. Isolated technical or physical exercises are inappropriate . Play a certain way – train a certain way.

Some coaches think that the best way to improve a team is by working fitness, technique, tactical and psychological components independently but under Tactical Periodization you cannot break these things apart – it is about the whole!

Chapter 5

Create habits through systemic repetition

"Systematic repetition [is] not the simple automation of a certain type of behaviour, but the understanding and learning of certain principles, so they become regularities." Frade (2003 mentioned by Freitas, S. in 2004)

The importance of emotions and feelings in the creation of habits

"Automatism, or habit as a result of knowledge, comes from mental images that were created through experience, conscious or unconscious, retained in the memory… used to support decisions and reactions to certain situations. Such a mechanism allows the subject to get rid of the basic elements of execution to concentrate on motor performances that are technically more complex and elevated." Damásio (2000 mentioned by Gaiteiro in 2006)

The daily functioning of the brain is based on two levels: the conscious and unconscious/subconscious. Most of the activity performed belongs to the unconscious level which, in a way, is more economical and functional, since the conscious one requires multiple brain structures to develop.
Furthermore, we can affirm that all decisions and actions are initiated by, and are a result of, subconscious activity (Gaiteiro 2006). Also, decisions and actions that happen in the game are initiated by, and the result of, subconscious activity.

According to McCrone (2002 mentioned by Gaiteiro 2006) "such subconscious processes that make decisions and fast reactions possible are denominated habits or automatisms."

This way, shortcuts are created, saving time through a specific setting of stimuli. So when the brain faces situations (in the game) identical or similar to the ones that has experimented with (during training) previously (that were incorporated as automatisms), it reacts unconsciously to certain known stimuli. This way, "decisional timing can be reduced from 500 to 200 milliseconds." as per Jensen (2002 mentioned by Gaiteiro 2006).

This mechanism allows the brain to dedicate more time to more complex technical performances, leaving the subconscious to take care of the basic elements of decision-making and execution, allowing the "neuronal ways to become more and more efficient" (Jensen, 2002 mentioned by Gaiteiro 2006).

In this decision-making mechanism, emotions and feelings play a crucial part. As confirmed by Damasio (in Descartes' Error) emotions and feelings act in the processes of reasoning and decision-making. As Denigot (2004 mentioned by Freitas 2004) makes clear "Our decisions hardly ever depend on reasoning."

In other words, feelings (thoughts generated through the consciousness of emotions) act unconsciously (generating positive or negative images of our body, to known stimuli, in our mind – somatic markers[10]; Damásio, A. (1995 mentioned

---

[10] These are a special case of feelings generated from secondary emotions. These emotions and feelings have been connected, through learning, to predictable future results in certain circumstances. When a negative somatic marker juxtaposes to a certain future result, the combination works as an alarm bell. But a positive somatic marker becomes a guide or incentive. Somatic markers do not decide for us. They help us decide by highlighting options and removing them from consequent consideration (Damásio 1994).

by Freitas, S. in 2004) "the memories of past emotions are reactivated by a neuronal circuit that takes into consideration the modifications connected to the emotion, and influence the final decision, diverting attention towards the consequences of such a decision or influencing the reason."

To Freitas (referncing Damásio 1995 in 2004), "Reasoning and normal decision-making imply that the decision maker (player) has knowledge of the situation that requires the decision, of the different response options, and the consequences of each of those options (results), immediately or in the future. It also implies that the decision maker has a logical strategy (principles) to produce valid inferences, which will help to select one valid response option, a sort of game plan chosen between several plans that were practiced in the past in countless situations and that provide the necessary support processes to reasoning... specific attention (tactical concentration), and the working memory." Damásio (2003 mentioned by Freitas 2004) clarifies this process further, and explains that a player, before making a decision, has two possibilities of action – knowledge and logic – that can go alone or complement each other, and a mechanism – emotion – that simplifies the work of reason.

So, we are saying that experiencing certain behaviours (principles and subprinciples of the game) creates emotions and feelings which, later on (prior to a similar situation in a game), will help us decode the information available to us, and make a decision, thus reducing the reasoning process, allowing us to anticipate events.

If experiencing a situation is how we reduce the reasoning process (i.e. we become faster at making decisions), Tactical Periodization promotes the experiencing of such situations through its specificity so that when we face similar experiences during competition, our anticipation skills are improved.

Create habits through systemic repetition (part 2)

"What Mourinho wants is for his concerns about moments of the game to be repeated, during training, lots of times, more than any other."
Amieiro, Oliveira, Resende, & Barreto (2006)

As reflected in previous chapters, what Tactical Periodization seeks to achieve is adaptation by the players to play in a certain way dictated by the coach, and for intentions (what we want to happen) to become actions during competition. As per Gomes (2006), "For the behaviours of the players and team to be inscribed automatically in the development of the playing project we must create habits… Through them, the behaviours arise at unconscious level, they result from the capacity to anticipate the response."

According to Frade (1998 mentioned by Rocha 2000) "When we train to achieve an adaptation, the process happens at the "know-how" level. To Carvalhal (2001) this adaptation is created "through a habit that is acquired in the action."

As per The Practical Illustrated Dictionary, Lello (mentioned by Carvalhal 2001), defines habit as an "acquired disposition through the frequent repetition of an action."

Bordieu (mentioned by Carvalhal 2001) adds that, "the disposition is a wider term than habit and can be defined as know-how… dispositions can be innate or acquired." and that "habit is an acquired disposition, where learning can take different shapes, and simple repetition is often insufficient."

This repetition can be, at times, insufficient because that habit, which is acquired in the action, can evolve (or not) with repetition. If the repetition of an action is active and contextualized, then there will be evolution, acquiring a new "know how." On the contrary, if the repetition is done in a non-active way, the acquired dispositions will remain but there will be no evolution.

Given the importance of systemic repetition in the transformation of a "know how" into a habit, Frade (mentioned by Carvalhal 2001) proposed the idea that "to acquire a principle, training must be acquisitive." Tactical Periodization is based on the Principle of Tendencies; in other words, it consists in creating a high incidence of what we want to achieve (the intended objective). To do so, we must determine the practice so the intended behaviour arises frequently.

The way to operationalize a principle, for the purpose of achieving adaptation by players, is through systemic (specific) repetition. Let's imagine that we want the players of our team to perform a certain type of pressure. We perform an exercise where six players are pressing - three attackers and three midfielders (in a 1-4-3-3 system), against a team of seven players in possession of the ball, for example four defenders and three midfielders. If we want players to adopt this principle of pressure we must set rules to the game so there are plenty of ball recoveries by the pressing players. The systemic repetition (recovering the ball) will thus become a habit. By making the habit specific to our vision of the game, we will be able to reach the sphere of "knowing about know-how." which is nothing else than "being aware of what we want." Frade (2007).

From "know-how" to "knowing about a know-how"

"To train in Specificity and to have the support of the viability of the acquisition of playing principles in systemic repetition, promotes the emergence of intentions, within the team, in the moment corresponding to previous intentions." Amieiro, Oliveira, Resende, & Barreto, (2006)

Systemic repetition (achieved through the Principle of Tendencies) is expanded upon by Frade and also by Resende when he tells us that, "learning (assimilating and owning certain principles of the playing model) comes from systemic repetition" which must be intentional and active; in other words, specific. As Carvalhal (2001) explains, "Besides repetition, learning requires an intentional structure of the repeated occurrences; their effects become more visible the more active the learning is." In other words, "only intentional movement is educational." Frade (mentioned by Freitas 2004)

We are saying that the habit we want to create in a player, through systemic repetition, must be intentional and contextualized in relation to the playing model.

That is why Frade (mentioned by Resende 2002) sees the "necessity of the emergence of the tactical-technical dimension in advance of the physical one." The tactical aspect must be the guide to the whole process, giving sense to the practice, and forcing the player to be mentally active. The tactical focus produces, in the player, a new acquisition belonging not only to the sphere of "know-how." but also to one of "knowing about know-how."

Even though it is true that training, through systemic repetition (fulfilling one of the main principles of the teaching-learning process), will be useful to acquire certain habits (e.g. know-how), it is fundamental that the acquisitive side we are talking about happens in a contextualized manner (specific), connected to the playing model. This creates a certain relationship between mind and habit that becomes fundamental when we try to transform "know-how" into a "knowing about know-how." something that becomes extremely important. As Le Moigne says, "In this model, the problem of decision-making in complex situations is conceived as a problem of qualitative representation, obliged to respond to the question of what to do, more than the one of how to do it.

Also, we must take into account that, in the current society we live in, there are lots of behaviours that are conditioned by culture, or the past of each individual, and that a team is formed by a large number of individuals, each one of them with their own ideas and ways of playing - depending on each situation demanded by the game. So the task of the coach will be to model the ideas of each of the individuals forming his team, and to make all of them think the same, and in the same way, for each situation. This will bring us to the sphere of "knowing about know-how" (Carvalhal, 2001).

Systemic repetition (in specificity)

"When I was 14 I could do any square root, I was tired of doing them at school. However, now that I have a degree I can hardly do one. The lack of practice made me forget them." Tamarit (2007)

Training must not be based only upon the acquisition of new principles but also in the maintenance of those already learnt. Players forget when they do not practice certain drills.

As Castelo (mentioned by Resende 2002) explains, "The lack of practice, of certain exercises, makes players/teams forget over time due to not using information retained in the memory and the instructions for its execution." He adds, "[lack of practice] brings a decrease in the capacity to perform actions with skill levels achieved previously."

For instance, a guitar apprentice begins practicing plucking with his guitar. Over time (more or less, depending on their learning skills), they will achieve ability with their fingers that allows them to increase the speed for playing the guitar strings. If, over three months, they stop plucking to practice strumming, when they try to pluck again their finger speed will have decreased considerably. Exactly the same thing happens to footballers; if they stop practicing tactical and tactical-technical actions, they will lose quality on their execution.

Training in specificity means that players do not forget the principles and subprinciples that form the playing model, because they are being constantly trained; the same happens to fundamental tactical-technical abilities. For Castelo (mentioned by Resende 2002) "Practicing specific training drills repeatedly and systematically helps players to evolve through the development of the different systems in the body, especially the central nervous system... To educate is not just to develop the muscles but to habituate the brain to command the body." He also adds, "Intelligence is a very important characteristic, since the athlete must have the cleverness to, firstly, observe and capture what he must do, then to be able to register it in his memory and immediately afterwards, send an order that can be obeyed by several muscle groups." The author gives high importance to the intelligence that the player must have and that, of course, must be given though the specificity that prevails in the training process.

Garganta (mentioned by Resende 2002) refers to this intelligence when he says that in football "it is not enough to reach further, jump higher, be stronger, it is necessary to be faster, quicker." To be quicker at thinking, at finding solutions, at finding the error and decoding the signals that surround it. Garganta & Pinto (mentioned by Resende 2002) add, "good players adjust themselves not only to the situations that they see but also to those that they anticipate, making decisions according to the probabilities of evolution of the game." To Castelo (mentioned by Resende 2002) "Knowledge and experience are leading factors in the elaboration of a perceptual process, a process that can only be developed with practice in the action."

Awakening feeling in training: a job for the coach

"Mourinho does not only try to create mental images – to record in the body the experiences connected to the game – but also to associate emotions and feelings that ease the decision-making process, using that brain tool called somatic markers." Amieiro, Oliveira, Resende, & Barreto, R., (2006)

If, as mentioned before, feelings are so important in the decision-making process, we understand that it is crucial to create emotions and feelings (somatic markers) during training. The coach shall be in charge of this.

According to Jensen (2002 mentioned by Freitas 2004) "reports from many scientists at the Center for the Neurobiology of Learning and Memory (CNLM) suggest there are better memory results from situations with high emotional excitement." Memory, somehow, remembers better the events that are associated with a high emotional load. "Emotions are inseparable from the idea of reward or punishment, pleasure or pain, approach or distance, personal advantage or disadvantage. Inevitably emotions are inseparable from the idea of good and bad." Damásio (2000)

We see that the intervention of the coach in each exercise, transmitting and creating emotions (negative or positive) to certain behaviours of his players, before certain specific situations of play, will influence future identical or similar situations to the ones already experienced, helping in the selection of choices. They will create certain regularities that will endow the team with an identity, since "[through]…positive emotions associated to behaviours that the coach demands for the playing model, and negative emotions to undesirable behaviors, the player realizes and feels good when he behaves according to the principles, subprinciples, and subprinciples of the subprinciples of the playing model" (Freitas 2004).

Summary

Brain functioning occurs at two levels: the conscious and unconscious (also referred to as the subconscious). Decisions and actions that happen in the game of football are typically initiated by, and the result of, unconscious/subconscious activity.

Somatic markers can be thought of as emotional feelings and associations that guide decision-making and behaviour. They are mental shortcuts which reduce our need to take time out to think about things. Experiences, underpinned by strong emotion, help us act - in similar situations - quickly. Because Tactical Periodization trains players under highly match-realistic circumstances - when players face similar experiences during competition, positive and negative somatic markers quickly guide their behaviour.

Coaches create "know how" in their players by exposing them to realistic situations which (literally) enables them to 'know how' to deal with a given scenario.

Tactical Periodization is based on the Principle of Tendencies; if we want to achieve something, we must practice it so the intended behaviour arises frequently. It's all about repetition, such that repetition breeds habit. Repetition must be intentional and active.

Through the tactical process underpinning training and repetition, players should start to 'know' about their know-how. It is not that they simply know what to do in a certain circumstance, they shall start to appreciate *why*. In turn, training is not just about learning new skills, previously learned ones must be maintained else they will be lost.

A number of commentators hold the role of intelligence in football highly. Players need intelligence, they argue, to assimilate and use information, as well as think and problem solve faster.

As a coach, it is your responsibility to train players so that they feel emotion and generate somatic markers. By associating emotions with behaviours, your players will be able to access previously rehearsed behaviours in future situations. If the team, as a whole does this, they will play with a particular identity.

Chapter 6

The team as a non-mechanistic mechanism

"Without details, without creativity, the game loses its richness. However, there is also a need for understanding… Because, that same creativity, that same detail must always be within a context, in a line of playing. That creativity and that detail cannot emerge anarchically, they must be related to the fulfillment of any given playing action. The question is this, how do you bring about that detail through analytic training? In my opinion it is impossible… they are jugglers that have certain abilities but always out of context" Faria (cited by Resende 2002)

"Imagine a student with a great capacity for dictation. Any dictated text is studied, written and rewritten by the student. Nothing is easier… not a single mistake. But he is asked to write an essay on a topic of his choice or one chosen by the teacher, will he do it as easily? We think that, at least, he is limited in his capacity to create or recreate, from the new context, what was presented to him. Versatility, malleability, spontaneity, invention, those are qualities that are not highly developed by him." Amieiro, Oliveira, Resende, & Barreto (2006)

Through systemic repetition, in a process based on specificity, we manage to create habits that will allow certain principles and subprinciples connected to the playing model, to regularly appear and anticipate action.

However, our aim is not to configure some 'mechanical' team. Our objective is to form a team with clear hierarchical rules, with unified principles, and where similar thinking, by a large number of team players, establishes a working logic that creates anticipation towards the action about to happen. Anticipation that marks the beginning of an action not an end. Anticipation allows more time to think about details, more time for creativity.

As Gomes (2006) says, "we try to habituate the player to resolve problems according to a logic, but the way of how he behaves, here and now, when settling the principles, cannot be mechanistic." For that, "Game principles can never be understood as a purpose itself, or as a stereotyped sequence of actions that present themselves as the manifestation of an unconscious solution – a closed mechanism" (as mentioned in Chapter 4), but instead they will be understood as "the beginning of a behavior that the coach wants the team to assume in collective terms as well as for the players in individual ones." Oliveira (2006 mentioned by Fonseca 2006). We want to allow players the freedom to create the final development of the action.

Therefore, there is a creativity that destroys the mechanism, transforming it into a "non-mechanistic mechanism." Even though it has some rules, it is unpredictable. To Oliveira (mentioned by Gomes 2006), "Details are key because they promote diversity and develop the team, the players, the coach and, consequently, the game."

If this creativity is so important, it should then be promoted during training.

The game: science and game

"The game has too much game to be science, and it is too scientific to be just a game." Frade (2005)

We have already spoken about football as a constructed phenomenon. Football is not a natural phenomenon. What we want to achieve, through Tactical Periodization, is the creation and implementation, through training, of principles and subprinciples that happen with certain regularity. Therefore, achieving a playing model: an identity that characterizes the game as something scientific. However, within these regularities, there is an uncontrollable and unexpected part - the part of detail and creativity.

To Mourinho (mentioned by Amieiro, Oliveira, Resende, & Barreto 2006), there is a "difference between the level of detail and the level of principles."

As per Frade (2004) "the highest quality of the top teams has too much game to be considered science, but on the other hand that game quality is too scientific to be just a game." In other words, great teams have a lot of diversity, a lot of detail (what we would call creativity), and this is the sphere of the game: the uncontrollable, unexpected side, which moves away from the scientific. Furthermore, that quality of the game is too scientific to be just a game, due to a number of irregularities that happen match after match.

In this way, we manage to differentiate two evident sides during the game. The scientific side based on the intended playing model, and the principles and subprinciples that shape it (the scientific side allows for something to be done under the same circumstances, by different people, and in the same way (repetition is needed in science)). And the non-scientific side, sustained through the detail, the creativity of the players. This part has no equivalence.

So, the game produced by a team has, within its regularities, the scientific part, because game after game it presents a behavior that is repeated (for instance how and when to press). And it has the non-scientific part in the detail and creativity, because it is something that happens randomly and and is not repeated.

Creativity: a disorder that only exists within an order

"Creativity only makes sense according to a playing idea that is called the playing model." Resende (2002)

As per Carvalhal (2001), "The team must be a non-mechanistic mechanism, where creative thinking is always present, at the time of deciding, at that unique moment, for which there is no calculation, an immeasurable foreseeability." However, for the author, this detail makes no sense without organization.

We must not forget that the organization of the game is essentially a system of permanent reorganization. Still, the quality of the game cannot be reduced to orderliness, even though it produces it, since it cannot get rid of disorder. A disorder that not only opposes order but, oddly, also cooperates with it to create organization.

Thus, if there is no creativity without order and there is no order without disorder, it is not coherent to separate these two sides.

However, this freedom/creativity appears as an outcome to growing complexity and not as its foundation. So we have to understand it as a dimension of the complex phenomenon that football is, because creativity in the game cannot be confused with "technicalities"; it must be connected to efficiency and to the aim of the game. As Oliveira says, "Creativity is not a circus, it is creativity according to something. Players need to understand that, what creativity is according to the team." Portolés (2007) goes the same way when he says that, "there cannot be creativity without intentionality."

We are then talking about creativity helping the group, helping the team. And creativity must be based on the playing model. Oliveira refers to that when he states, "creativity during playing must be rationalized and must be referred to the implemented playing model and the model of player."

Based on all the previous comments, this creativity, this detail, must not be reduced during training; it must arise from the principles and subprinciples that form the Playing Model. It must be contextualized into the play.

We will achieve this if we manage to operationalize it during training. In other words, creativity/freedom is only achieved when we live it. This experience of intentional creativity, that we aim for, must happen during training. It will hardly happen if training is analytic and out of the game's context.

The importance of anticipation in the process of creativity

"Anticipation is what gives life to creativity. Without anticipation there cannot be creativity." Portolés (2007)

As the neuroscientist Antonio Damásio wrote: "images allow us to select the repertoires of actions previously available and to optimize the execution of the chosen action. This way we can automatically receive mental images representing different options, different backgrounds, and different results of the action. We can select the most adequate actions and reject the rest. The source of transforming and combining images of actions and backgrounds is the source of all creativity." In other words, it is all about anticipating action through the knowledge of the different results that might come about depending on the decision we make. This knowledge allows us to select the ideal decision. To achieve this knowledge we must have previous experiences related to the image we are receiving.

We must create, henceforth, a training regime that works with the creativity/freedom we are talking about. We experience it within the playing model that we want to achieve and in the principles and subprinciples that give shape to it.

Tactical Periodization: a process of training that demands creativity

"We think that there is a more effective place for this freedom in Tactical Periodization than in Physical Periodization." Resende (2002)

The progressive overvaluation of "tactic-ism" in football, alongside a lack of street football, has created players who are fixed to the tactical roles given to them, losing creativity and intuition. If we wish to develop football, it is absolutely necessary to introduce creativity/freedom in the game. In other words, to create teams that are "non-mechanistic mechanisms."

Tactical Periodization seems to dedicate more time and space for the emergence of creativity (based on specific playing) than other training methodologies, because it works with it within the drills, within the intended playing model. As we stated in Chapter 4, principles mark the beginning of a behavior, not the end of it, and this is where the creativity of the player arises.

By constantly training the principles and subprinciples of the game, we integrate creativity/freedom into the training process. Creativity will emerge in situations of unpredictability, and because we are training with game simulations this unpredictability will have a greater presence than in analytic and closed training. This way, we get players to experience unpredictability as much as possible, making creativity emerge; and, as Damásio, made reference to, it helps achieve more accurate decision-making in the future, given the previous knowledge we have of the possible different results.

To Carvalhal (2001), "[whoever] follows the path of Tactical Periodization, must give priority to a certain order that will be optimized, updated through specific -exercises according to the mentioned playing model and its principles." but "creative thinking must always be present and, when deciding, that unique moment in which there is no reckoning, an incalculable predictability results, in practice, into a potential unpredictability... a result of the potential experiences undergone during the training process."

However, it must be clear what experience means. As Portolés (2007) comments, "sometimes we confuse experience with the simple fact of being in a place or acting or behaving based on standards... experience does not directly infer knowledge. The experience is a behavior in a certain situation, but for that behavior to really provide knowledge and an internal association of what you have practiced, and what you want to achieve, it needs the capability to interfere in the player's thinking. If the player simply acts in a game situation. this will not generate any direct knowledge or adaptation to a superior behavior."

To the author, "We must work anticipation and imagination abundantly. Imagination is seeing in our mind what is not yet real, what is yet to happen." To him, "this is achieved through experience and reflection."

We must make our players think, because "a person will easily use something he understands than something he does not. This is the sense of feeling, the sense of association that we have between knowledge and emotions. It is not about thinking about the movement you made just after you made it, it is about you being conscious of why you do it while you are doing it, even rectifying it if necessary at that very moment."

Summary

Through repeated training, we aim to develop a team which operates under rules and unified principles. These rules and principles allow the team to anticipate events, and anticipation creates time to think and be creative. Creativity is to be encouraged because it makes teams unpredictable.

There is too much 'game' in football for it to be science, but it is too scientific to be thought of as just a game. The scientific part is the repeatable behaviours a player or team may exhibit, whilst the non-scientific part is the creativity and detail that happens.

For creativity to occur, it needs to exist within an organising structure, and that structure is the playing model. In turn, there cannot be creativity without intentionality. It does not magic out of thin air, it has to be a deliberate characteristic.

Creativity needs to be practised during training. More than that, it is intentional creativity that must be practised (and always within a realistic game context). Players should also show imagination; imagination is derived from experience and reflection.

Previous experiences (by players and teams) combined with anticipation help drive creativity. Players need to experience different situations to form the knowledge base that allows them to problem solve and make decisions. Training regimes should work to deliver creativity and player freedom, all within the playing model. Fixed, analytical, and by-the-numbers training programmes do not provide the unpredictability needed to drive creativity.

Experiencing different situations does not simply mean 'being there'. It means being actively involved so that the experience affects the person.

Chapter 7

Training and concentration

"Running for the sake of it has a natural energetic wear, but the complexity of this exercise is null, and as such, the wear in emotional terms tends to also be null, unlike the complex situations where technical, tactical and physical requisites are demanded of the players, where they have to think about situations, that is what represents the complexity of the exercise and leads to a higher concentration." Mourinho (mentioned by Freitas, S. in 2004)

The Importance of concentration

"High performance football demands players to have a constant tactical awareness, in the game and also in training. It is necessary that what they do, they do in a focused way. For this, good performances during training demands a high level of concentration to achieve what the coach wants." Frade (2003 mentioned by Gaiteiro 2006)

As per Orlick (1986 mentioned by Freitas 2004), concentration is the "ability of each of us to direct our attention to the most relevant aspects of the task."

To other authors such as Schmid & Peper (1991 mentioned by Morilla, Pérez, Gamito, Gómez, Sánchez, and Valiente, 2002) "concentration is a learnt skill, to react passively or to not get distracted by irrelevant stimuli." In addition, they add, "concentration also means to be totally in the here and now, in the present." According to Silverio & Srebro (2002 mentioned by Freitas 2004), "concentration includes two elements: 1) The ability to pay attention to pertinent information and to ignore irrelevant and disruptive stimuli. 2) The ability to stay focused during a long period of time (90 minutes plus extra time)."

The importance that concentration acquires in competition is evident. As per Orlick & Nidefeer (1986 and 1991 mentioned by Freitas 2004), "Concentration is a decisive factor during competition, in collective and individual sports." To Morilla, Pérez, Gamito, Gómez, Sánchez, J. and Valiente (2002) "Concentration is one of the essential aspects for an athlete to achieve their potential maximum level."

We can verify such importance through different interviews with professional players and coaches where everyone agrees it is essential for success. Amongst them we highlight one from Luis Fernando Tena, coach of Club America in Mexico, when he talked about the importance of concentration for success in reference to their Club World Cup game against F.C. Barcelona, "We are facing a perfect team, always playing with the maximum concentration."

It is clear that we all give high importance to concentration in football. However, it is not an aspect that is practiced, and if done, it is done in a non-specific way, and it does not produce the ability to stay focused for a long period of time (in our case at least 90 minutes) on a task.

Our thinking prompts us to accept that concentration must be trained, and must be worked through the training process. To De le Vega (2003) in the absence of concentration during the game, "we should study and analyse the conditions in which the players train, because if they are only required to stay focused for a short period of time, it is then expected that during the game concentration will also fail (what we train gets reflected in competition)."

"Decisional concentration" (tactical) demanded in "Tactical Periodization" (thanks to specificity)

"Working and operating the playing model implies concentration." Faria (2002 mentioned by Freitas 2004)

The concentration we are talking about, and which we want to work during training, is not a general concentration but a specific concentration about a way of playing, so we will call it "tactical" or "decisional" concentration. This "tactical concentration" must be present in each of the drills performed during the process.

To Frade (2000 mentioned by Freitas 2004), "Tactical Periodization emphasizes the assimilation of a way of playing, its principles: organization of the defence; organization of the attack; and the other principles that are its boundaries, this is, how you move from one moment to another, these being done only through concentration." In other words, players need specific concentration for a certain way of playing.

Oliveira (mentioned by Freitas 2004) follows the same line and talks about specific concentration when he states that, "working our way of playing demands a certain type of concentration… we manage training for that way of playing so that it will be evidence of our game, and we intend for that concentration, the need to play in a certain way, to be also trained." According to the author, "concentration is one of the things you train so, in the game, we play better and achieve what we intend to do."

It is difficult then for this specific concentration, demanded by our playing model, to happen through analytic training. Mourinho (mentioned by Freitas 2004) refers to this when he says that, "It is the build-up of drills which demands that same concentration, and the drills demanded are not analytic ones but drills where the players have to think a lot; drills of increasing difficulty that oblige them to a permanent concentration."

Consequently, it will be through Tactical Periodization (thanks to its specificity) that we will manage to work with the required concentration in competition. To Carvalhal (mentioned by Freitas 2004), "the best way to boost that concentration is through situations that simulate our way of playing... simulation through drills, training big and small principles according to those four moments, is in my opinion, the only way to train concentration, at least at an operational level."

So, as we already explained, "concentration must always be present in training, but not any concentration... it must show up as a contextualized sub dimension within the training process, its operationalization. It must be a concentration related to the playing culture that the coach wants for his team... the only apparent way of bringing about that concentration seems to be through the specificity of the training, through the drills performed within a tactical-technical regime, taking into account the principles, subprinciples and subprinciples of the subprinciples of the playing model implemented by the coach," Freitas (2004).

The intervention of the coach in the search for the specific concentration

"Sometimes, the drills are completely adequate to the playing model, however, due to the inadequate intervention of the coach they may become misaligned." Oliveira (2004 mentioned by Gomes 2006)

The intervention of the coach is essential for achieving concentration during training. According to Oliveira (mentioned Freitas 2004) for, "Specificity to be truly acquired it is not enough for the drills to be specific in terms of the structure of the drills, it is necessary for the coach to intervene to enhance the specificity." Stressing the importance of the coach, it is the leader who corrects and explains possible errors and rewards the virtues shown by the team depending on the playing model that he wants to achieve. Schinke & da Costa (mentioned by Portolés 2006) refer to this when they explain, "according to Bandura, elite athletes require persuasion and specific technical feedback by accredited coaches in order to transcend their own perceived limits, to achieve results of the highest level and consequently confirm results."

To achieve this concentration, then, we must stand out through emotional orientation the behaviour we want in a drill, with the intervention of the coach as discussed in Chapter 5. It is clear how important the coach's intervention is, for the acquisition of the principles and subprinciples inherent to the desired playing model, as well as to the demands of specific concentration of such model in the drills, managing to transform "know how" into "knowing about know how."

According to Carvalhal (mentioned by Freitas 2004), "We are talking about a way of training, where this way of training is a simulation of reality, where we want moments of maximum intensity and for these maximum intensity situations to happen there must be concentration, so, we must focus to perform those types of actions."

Summary

Concentration is about not being distracted; it is about being in the 'here and now' and paying attention to important and relevant stimuli. It is also about keeping up this mental 'focus' over a long period of time.

Concentration is essential if an athlete wants to achieve their full potential.

Concentration is rarely practised in football, and if it is – it is often non-specific and for short periods. Tactical concentration is what we seek in football… for 90 minutes plus; it needs to be practised in all training exercises.

A coach's intervention is essential for developing player concentration during training. In turn, elite athletes require encouragement and specific technical feedback to achieve results of the highest level.

Chapter 8

Tactical Fatigue

"The most important fatigue in football is central nervous fatigue and not the physical one. Any professional team minimally trained on the energetic point of view manages to resist the game, with more or less difficulty. Now, central nervous fatigue is what results from permanently concentrating and, for example, from reacting immediately and in a coordinated way to the moment when possession of the ball is lost." Mourinho (2003 mentioned by Amieiro, Oliveira, Resende, Barreto 2006)

"Tactical fatigue" and physical fatigue: an interconnection that must not be understood separately

"We are not tired. It is not about fitness training but about concentration." Zambrotta (19th of January 2007 on Súper Deporte)

As per the previous chapter, we understand that Tactical Periodization demands concentration at all times during training, given the specificity the process is based on. There is also the concentration demanded by competition, and we see a type of "mental-emotional" fatigue which needs to be taken into account during recovery.

As per Silvério & Srebro (2002 mentioned by Freitas 2004), "Maintaining concentration over a long time implies effort and, as such, it is tremendously exhausting." Ferreira (2004 mentioned by Freitas 2004) proposed that, "the higher the concentration levels are, the higher the wear is."

Oliveira (2004 mentioned by Freitas 2004) also agrees with this. However, he goes a bit further when he suggests that mental fatigue can be higher than physical fatigue,

"Concentration sometimes is more exhausting than the game itself, in physiological terms, that is why what often leads to tiredness is concentration itself." Neca (2004 mentioned by Freitas 2004) agrees and affirms, "psychological wear is deeper than the physical one."

Given these statements, recovery must be in balance between two different levels: the "mental-emotional" level and the physical one (although these would not exist without total connection and interdependence; Amieiro, Oliveira, Resende, and Barreto 2006).

"Tactical Fatigue": "a problem of habituation"

"The psychological impact of a drill implies the unpleasant perception of fatigue, preceding the appearance of a physiological limitation in the muscles. This fatigue is produced in the Central Nervous System, since the activation of the muscles depends, partly, on the control of consciousness." Costill (1994 mentioned by Carvalhal 2001)

As per Duarte (1989 mentioned by Carvalhal 2001), "Fatigue is the incapacity to maintain a certain intensity of exercising, characterized by a reduction, more or less accentuated, in the functional ability of the player."

However, as mentioned earlier, the fatigue we refer to is not the generally understood fatigue, but instead it is a fatigue with a specific character derived from the specific situations from the desired playing model.

As Frade (1998 mentioned by Rocha 2000) tells us, "central nervous fatigue is one of the problems in collective sports." Adding that such fatigue "is characterized by the inability to concentrate, and to save effort resulting in a loss of understanding of the game."

Tactical Periodization has the virtue of increasing a player's capacity to concentrate through training, also, the creation of habits enabled by this process allows for acquired knowledge to become a part of the subconscious, reducing the use of the central nervous system, as stated in Chapter 5. Frade (mentioned by Carvalhal in 2001) refers to this with the following example, "it is like when someone reads a book, and after half an hour needs to rest. But is also possible that someone that never reads has a headache for a week." It is fundamentally a problem of habituation.

Important aspects to take into account in specific training with regards to concentration

"The manifestations of the mental load are the last ones to recover if the demands of the game were high." Platonov (1988 mentioned by Carvalhal 2001)

Given this type of fatigue, technical staff must always take concentration into account, or even better, the possible negative consequences that fatigue produced by this accumulation of concentration can carry if planning does not respect the restraining effect. We should worry about central nervous fatigue because to be focused for a long time can have negative effects.

This type of psychological wear (mental fatigue) is due, on occasion, to the elevated synchronism (repetition of drills) of movements between all the elements of the team, and can generate (due to routine) a loss of concentration and application. Prevention is needed to avoid getting negative results. Frade (1998 mentioned by Carvalhal in 2001) says that, "It is more important to prevent than to correct, through a continuous control of the situation, through dialogue, paying lots of attention to the behaviour of the player during training."

A key part of this prevention is based on the coach's need to understand that sometimes players cannot perform a drill properly, not due to a lack of interest but instead due to "mental-emotional" tiredness (which diminishes their ability to perform). The coach must realize the existence of "tactical fatigue" before a downturn in the attention and concentration of his players, with the resulting decrease of intensity in the execution of the work, so he can intervene at that exact moment, diversifying the work, varying the times and modes of the drills, without altering their objectives (even doing more entertaining drills if necessary).

But is not only about preventing and changing the drill at the moment we detect the "tactical fatigue." we must also do it through the planning of the training, taking into account the amount and type of concentration required to achieve, each day, the pattern morfocycle. The drills must also take into account the degree of complexity in concentration (that will provoke different adaptations in players' bodies).

In response to this, Frade (2000 mentioned by Resende 2002) explains, "In the same way that a player does an important job one day, it may not make sense to do it again the next day, it has no benefit, because to perform a training process it is necessary to select and fulfil the restraining effect, to emphasize certain reality. If the time separating an identical effort from another one is not enough to allow the player to rest, not only will the desired effect not happen but you will also end up with tired players."

The attitude of the coach also becomes very important at the time of balancing the intensity of the activity (since it must always be the maximum intensity). Intensity can be achieved with the right level of motivation; a positive attitude is related to an increase in the intensity of the drill, and vice versa. According to Mourinho (2004 mentioned by Freitas 2004), "With drills that demand concentration and in the presence of some central nervous fatigue, a link to a highly motivational factor can compensate, I think." Jensen (2002 mentioned by

Freitas 2004) follows the same path and explains, "The belief of the players in the content (playing model) and contexts (methodology) is essential as a controlling factor for motivation." The author adds, "We must wrap the players in a dream with high objectives."

The duration of training must not exceed 90 minutes, as Castelo (2000 mentioned by Carvalhal 2001) says, when the training is specific, "I can only train for an hour and a half, and the recovery will be necessarily part of the training, I cannot force the player to have a set of attitudes and behaviours that will collapse again the same nervous system."

It is clear then that we must plan training, keeping in mind the restraining effect, altering the exigency and type of concentration along the week. This does not mean that the intensity of concentration will not be the highest, as it should be for each training session, but that the complexity of an exercise from one day to another will vary. This way the players will always work at a maximum relative intensity, but the demand of concentration will not always be the same, because the degree of complexity of the drill will not always be the same.

We also see that a key way to motivate players is by making them believe in the playing model and in the process to follow, as well as maintaining a constant dialogue with them, preventing the appearance of "tactical fatigue" as much as possible, and modifying and altering the training if necessary. Lastly, we must understand that a training in specificity demands high loads of concentration, so it must not exceed 90 minutes, which includes breaks between repetitions and drills. We will only perform daily training, and allow the player to recover for the next training session where we will demand maximum concentration (relative maximum intensity).

Summary

Tactical fatigue stems from concentrating hard. For a player to maintain his or her concentration over a long time requires effort; and that is hugely tiring.

Some commentators feel that psychological fatigue is actually more draining than physical fatigue.

Psychological wear should be prevented rather than cured. Prevention can be achieved by monitoring players, talking to them, and paying attention to their behaviour. Sometimes a player cannot perform a drill properly because they are mentally and/or emotionally knackered. To prevent tiredness, coaches can change the time of practices, their focus, their complexity and more – but should not alter overall objectives.

Aside from seeing when players are becoming tired, coaches should also *anticipate* tiredness and factor it into their wider training planning. Coaches should pay attention to not necessarily repeating the same drills the day after one another.

Motivation is highly related to fatigue. If players are motivated, fatigue can be overcome.

Intensity should always be at the maximum during training but if players are tired, reduce the complexity of the session. Training sessions should not exceed 90 minutes. Players need time to recover after every training session so that they deliver maximum concentration and intensity at the next training session.

Chapter 9

The intensity and volume of performance

"The indiscriminate use of a term would not be serious if the words were not an instrument for analysing reality. But they are. Their meanings indicate open paths in the things that make them passable. A lost word is, perhaps, access to the lost reality. A blurry word is a hidden path through the undergrowth." Marina (1995 mentioned by Portolés 2006)

"When we talk about intensity, we refer to intensity of concentration, when we talk about volumes, we refer to volumes of intensity of concentration." Faria (2002 mentioned Resende 2002)

Intensity = Tactical Concentration

"The maximum fractions of cumulative intensity also mean the maximum fractions of intensity in cumulative concentration." Carvalhal (2001)

With Tactical Periodization we must begin by understanding the terms volume and intensity from a different perspective to the commonly known. Understanding these terms is key because, in our process, we must work from the very first day with maximum relative intensities.

To Oliveira (mentioned by Freitas 2004), maximum relative intensity "is the necessary intensity to successfully perform a certain type of action." We see in its definition that we are talking about an intensity based on the level of mental demand. As referred to by Amieiro, Oliveira, Resende & Barreto (2006), "the intensity will be determined by the mental-emotional weariness of a performance and not by the action of movement." We refer to an intensity related to decisions, therefore associated to concentration ("tactical concentration").

Also, to Faria, (mentioned by Resende 2002) "intensity is essentially about concentration, mainly because the game involves thinking, and thinking demands to be focused, and demanding to be focused is a high level demand... which is fundamental for our game, the way the coach wants the team to play. Having the capacity to remain focused as much as possible implies a certain capacity of concentration and the capacity to hold on as long as possible implies a certain volume of intensity of concentration."

Frade (1998 mentioned by Rocha 2000) points out, "Intensity is only characterized when associated with concentration," and that, "a slower drill can be way more intense if it implies a certain articulation that requires more concentration." Carvalhal (2001) provides an example: "If we want to run a distance at maximum speed, we will do it with high intensity. However, if we want to do that same distance carrying a tray full of glasses, doing that as quickly as possible without dropping any glasses, inevitably this second action, even though slower, will be more intense because it requires higher concentration." So, "this last drill becomes slower inasmuch as it demands more concentration, the relevance of the implied structure is a perceptual-kinetic relevance."

Likewise, Oliveira (mentioned by Freitas 2004) affirms that intensity, "can be standing still or can be at high speed, it depends on the situation, so the important thing is the intensity." To him, "relative maximum intensity must permanently complement training because we must always do things so that we succeed... what matters is to understand that relative maximum intensity is related to what one needs to do, that is why it is related to the tactical dimension, which in turn is related to the technical dimension, the psychological dimension and the cognitive dimension. It is related to all those dimensions."

Intensity then, only makes sense if it is connected to concentration, and concentration will be more demanding the more variables it encompasses. That is why a slower drill that implies a certain articulation (between principles and subprinciples) can be way more intense, because it demands high levels of concentration.

In other words, we can say that the connection between intensity and concentration is established by the notion of specificity (our playing model). We are then facing an intensity that is not abstract. To Frade (2007), in order to have intensity we must work in "real time."

Volume = accumulated fractions of relative maximum intensity

We will talk about a volume of relative maximum intensities (a volume of principles and subprinciples of the game), which is to say, a volume generated through the repetition of drills in maximum relative intensity seeking to acquire the principles and subprinciples that will give shape to our playing model. It is a volume of specificities.

To Frade (2000 mentioned by Resende 2002) "the volume must be the volume of intensities, this is, the growth or increase of the intensities that I am interested in," and not the volume as the amount of work. So, for the author, "the purpose of the increase in training volume will be to provide recoveries. And what is the result of this? The body gets used to being in those circumstances, it gets tired when it is requested to do effort, but in terms of that kind of effort it recovers faster to be able once again to make another effort." Garganta (1991 mentioned by Carvalhal in 2001) supports this idea, "work should emphasize intensity."

So it is this succession of high intensity fractions that take us to an accumulated intensity, an intensity related to the playing model. In the words of Carvalhal (2001), "this volume of maximum intensities (relate to the adopted playing model) grows gradually over the season to achieve a level that we consider optimum for our team, keeping it till the end." It will grow because the recovery times get smaller and smaller.

The achievement of a performance level: stabilization at the expense of progression

"I don't want my team to have performance peaks... I couldn't want the performance of my team to change! I always want my team in high performance levels. Because there are no games or periods more important than others..." Mourinho (2006 mentioned by Amieiro, Oliveira, Resende, & Barreto 2006)

According to Amieiro, Oliveira, Resende & Barreto (2006) "The balance of an optimal performance level is achieved when institutionalising a weekly training pattern – related to content, recovery, regimes, the number and duration of the training units – and its stabilization." To the authors, "it is about building a weekly dynamic and keeping it over the season, from the preparatory period (preseason)."

So it is about creating a weekly working dynamic and keeping it up from the beginning, from preseason, until the end of the season. This is another principle that forms Tactical Periodization.

Under this perspective, Mourinho (2006 mentioned by Amieiro, Oliveira, Resende,& Barreto 2006) says that it must be worked from day one of preseason "at relative maximum intensities, associated to the specificity in our game." He adds that he does not believe in an "increase of volume or inverting volume for intensity."

Tactical Periodization, based on the principle of stabilization, is trained from the first day of the second week (since week one is for adaptation to the specific effort of the game) at relative maximum intensities, since it demands concentration for the acquisition of principles and subprinciples, as well as their implementations, which will give shape to the intended playing model. The workload (referring to amount) stays the same, from the second week to the last, with increased intensity and reduced recovery time as the training process advances.

To Resende (mentioned by Gaiteiro, B 2006) "the volume of playing principles is similar every week, and by becoming regular it will be the core of the play, expressing the collective growth."

This is how we achieve playing at a level of optimal and specific performance, suitable to our way of playing. Relative maximum intensities from the very first day of training, identical workloads, and a weekly working pattern, based on the principles and subprinciples that shape the playing model - repeated from the second week.

However, despite the weekly pattern being similar from the second week to the final week, "they are not copies but replicas and reflections from one another, showing small modifications in play." (Gaiteiro 2006). He adds that, "the system is constituted of isomorphic replicas of the basic model." that is why it gets the name of Morphocycle. This equality in Morphocycles allows for stability. Stability is seen as "the regular manifestation of regularities." (Gaiteiro 2006).

It is obvious then that the biggest concern during preseason, with Tactical Periodization, is getting the team to play in a certain way, achieving, due to the specificity that this implies, an ideal level in all factors. It will be through the Morphocycle Pattern, worked from the second week of training to the last, that we will reach an optimal level of performance; we will achieve the stabilization that Tactical Periodization preaches, moving away from unwanted peaks of form.

Summary

We should not confuse work (and work-rate) as some high-energy activity (e.g. running around a lot); high level work is about carrying out high intensity tasks. A high intensity football task might actually involve barely any movement at all.

A high intensity task (such as a particular football drill) might be physically slow because the variables being explored are complex and therefore need to be run through at a particular pace.

Highly intense tasks can be grouped into a 'volume' of tasks/drills. In turn, the volume of maximum intensity drills may, or may not, be increased (in a session, for example) as the season progresses and players become acclimatised to this kind of work. The time they need to recover between intensities will diminish over a season.

The workload (i.e. the amount of work) stays the same across the season, though. It is the volume of intensities that can gradually increase. In other words, you do not add more hours to the training programme, you add more high intensity drills until you find the optimum level for the team. The actual working pattern of any programme should stay the same across the weeks.

Teams should always seek to deliver high intensity work because there are no periods in the game that are more important than others. You do not train your team to concentrate more at one point, then throttle back at other times. They must remain maximally focused throughout.

An important element to Tactical Periodization is the idea that the weekly working dynamic must be established from day one of preseason. Training players to operate at maximum relative intensity starts at the very beginning of the programme. No building them up slowly. A stable training programme is key.

Chapter 10

A weekly training pattern in search of stabilization: The Morphocycle Pattern

The weekly pattern is key to the organization of the process, since after the game, it analyses and defines a set of goals to work on during the week." Gomes, M. (2006 referring to Oliveira)

The Morphocycle Pattern: work made game by game

"Training is the principal way to create the competition and the game that we want… the competition is also very important because it gives us direction to reshape what we do during training." Oliveira (mentioned by Gomes 2006)

To Oliveira (mentioned by Gomes 2006) and opening this chapter: "The weekly pattern is key to the organization of the process since after the game, it analyses and defines a set of goals to work on during the week."

For him, the morphocycle pattern of a week is carried out with the intention of "preparing for the next game, taking into account what happened in the previous match, and what is expected for the next one." That is why the author states, "training is the primary means to create the competition and the game we want."

Mourinho (mentioned by Gaiteiro 2006) talks about the same thing when he says, "training, in each and every circumstance… must always be closely related to what we want for the game (thus specific). That is why, when I plan the working week, I do it in advance and in a comprehensive way, taking into account my main playing principles. Afterwards, depending on what I believe will be necessary for the next game (a tactical-strategic concern from where adaptability emerges), I finalize the planning of the week."

So, the planning of a morphocycle must relate to the game the team produces, the game the team played last match, and (last but not least) the game we want to occur in the next match. The days we have between games are of extreme importance, and cause the morphocycle pattern to vary.

Principles of the Morphocycle Pattern's formation

"The Morphocycle Pattern is ruled by three principles: the Principle of Complex Progression, the Principle of Propensities, and the Principle of Specific Horizontal Alternation... the Principle of Principles is Specificity." Frade (2005)

As we have been saying throughout this book, the concerns of "Tactical Periodization" are based on the 'play', so the purpose behind training is always tactical, based on the desired playing model, completing the principle of principles: specificity.

However, in the creation of a morphocycle pattern, in addition to the principle of specificity, we also have "three principles or methodological pillars: the principle of complex progression, the principle of specific horizontal alternation, and the principle of propensities" (Frade 2004 mentioned by Gaiteiro 2006).

The first Principle that Vítor Frade talks about is related to progression, which, as per Gaiteiro (2006), "means the need to prioritize the principles… avoiding interference and concurrence between them. A hierarchical experience from the acquisitive point of view." In other words, we try to reduce the complexity of the playing model, so that principles and subprinciples will be more complex as players understand them better. They will even be modified depending on the needs of the moment. Certain principles and subprinciples will be pushed over others, since not all of them have the same relevance.

The second principle, the principle of propensities, which we have already talked about, is about repeating aspects that we want our players to acquire (systemic repetition), as mentioned on Chapter 5.

The third and final principle is the one called the principle of specific horizontal alternation. It is necessary to have a horizontal alternation... of intensity, duration and speed, where specificity still remains. As per Gaiteiro (2006), "this alternation happens horizontally along the morphocycle." It is horizontal because "it results from alternating what is central between trainings and not between drills in one session." This prevents overtraining from appearing.

This is the principle in charge of regulating the relationship between effort and recovery. According to Resende (mentioned by Gaiteiro 2006) - in biological terms, it is not possible for a body to deliver constantly the same effort, every day. Thus, the different principles and subprinciples must be classified, training the ones that work on the same structures on the same day, and avoiding overdoing things during the week effort-wise. The structures already trained need time to rest and regenerate.

As Gomes (2006) says, we can easily see how we need to approach the top principles or subprinciples, because different efforts prevail and so, each level of organization works in a certain schedule of demands. In this way, we alternate the efforts from one day to another in the morphocycle pattern. Otherwise, as the author states, if we work on the same things on different days of the week we promote an incorrect effort-recovery relationship because there is an overload on the same structures.

Morphocycle Pattern with a weekly game (Sunday to Sunday)

"Daily, we train the principles and the interactions between principles, regarding the defensive and offensive organization, as well as transitions after loss or recovery of the ball, corresponding to the playing model."
Gaiteiro (2006)

As we have already mentioned in this book, the morphocycle pattern will be identical from the second week to the final week, because the first week will be of adaptation, each session lasting 90 minutes, with one single session per day (due to recovery needs). The principles and subprinciples will vary from session to session, accomplishing the principle of specific horizontal alternation and the principle of complex progression, respecting the recovery of certain structures already worked.

For a Team playing just one competition (Sunday to Sunday), the morphocycle pattern would be as follows:

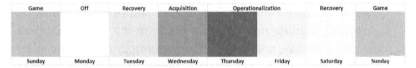

Graphic adapted from Oliveira.

Monday. Passive recovery.

This is the first day off for the team. It happens the day after competing, and even though it is not the best option from a physiological point of view, it is the best from the mental perspective; as we have been saying in previous chapters, we

92

must take mental fatigue into account, especially since Tactical Periodization involves constantly working on concentration.

As per Mourinho (2006 mentioned by Gaiteiro 2006) training the day after the game "is better for the 'body' but worse for the head." So, in Tactical Periodization we take the day off following a game.

Tuesday. Day of sub-dynamic active-recovery.

On Tuesday, recovery is still present, but it is active. Training must have frequent rest stops. In other words, it must be discontinuous, and allow players time to recover. The specificity principle is present in the whole morphocycle pattern so it is no exception on this day; we promote principles and subprinciples under a recovery regime.

To Frade (2007) this day continues to target "recovery".

As per Oliveira (2006 mentioned by Gomes 2006) "this day approaches some subprinciples that we understand must be 'trained' in relation to what happened during the previous game (good or bad) and what we foresee will be the next game." This means, we either work on aspects from the previous game, or we strategically work with a focus on the next game (without forgetting that the important thing is our way of playing). In essence, we prepare for the next game from the first day of training. The author clarifies that, "it promotes a characteristic effort of a game but with a high reduction of the speed, tension and duration..." But it is not only about the reduction of the training in all its aspects (tension, duration and speed) but also of concentration, reducing the complexity of the training (which *does not* mean to stop working at relative maximum intensities). It means creating situations without opposition or without a high degree of difficulty (Gomes 2006).

We are talking about a recovery specific to the playing model, based on the principles and subprinciples, where the recovery of concentration is respected, and exercises are not overly complex.

Players who did not take part in the previous game must have more challenging work, in every aspect.

An example of an exercise on a day of active recovery could be the 11 players who played the game replicating the movements that went well during the game, against a team consisting of 6 players (who did not compete). This way we work a great principle - the positioning of the team and ball circulation, during our recovery regime. We could also work on the circulation of the ball that we want to do for the next match (depending on the type of defense that we will face in the next match; a tactical-strategic regime).

Wednesday. Day of sub-dynamic tension.

On Wednesday, we work on the subprinciples of the game. However, demands are different from the competition (since players are still not fully recovered three days after the game), with more recovery time, reduced spaces, higher muscle contraction speeds, and reduced groups of players. As per Mourinho (2006 mentioned by Gaiteiro 2006) "experience tells me that three days after the game the players are still not fully recovered. Not so much in physical terms but, fundamentally, in emotional terms. The emotional exhaustion takes longer than the physical to recover."

As per Oliveira (2006 mentioned by Gomes 2006) on this day "we create situations with a relatively small number of players, reduced spaces and the duration of training is also reduced."

According to Frade (2007) it is about distinguishing the situations that require higher effort, the ones with greater chances to experience higher acceleration or deceleration, changes of direction. This is replicating the moments of action with eccentric contractions whether they are related to attacking or defending."

A Wednesday training exercise could involve 4 defenders (defence sector) performing defensive work against 6 players, 3 strikers plus 3 midfielders (inter-sector midfield-attack) who try to score. The work must be very intermittent because the demand on the defenders is very high… it demands lots of situations with changes of direction, pulls, jumps, etc. Since the inter-sector midfield-attack is doing a less demanding job, they combine their actions with small sided games of 3vs3 in triangles (referring to the playing model) with finishing on goal, where plenty of situations of a similar type of those performed by the defenders happen, as well as lots of shots on goal.

Thursday. Day of sub-dynamic duration.

Being the furthest from the day of the last game and the closest to the next game, on Thursday we work the main principles (the collective dynamic of the team) with demands similar to the ones on the day of competition. This way we work in big spaces, with longer time duration and with more players. It is, in essence, training that is closer to the reality of competition.

To Frade (2007) it is the most intense day "because I increase the spaces and I focus on greater principles… the duration of implementation can be longer as well as the space. Therefore, concentration demands are bigger, as well as the emotional investment (emotional exhaustion)."

Oliveira (2006 mentioned by Gomes 2006) advises to "work benefiting the main principles or some subprinciples that are related to those main principles." To him, "the dynamic of these situations promotes an effort very similar to the one desired in competition." This day "we train the articulations of the sectors with most or all of the team."

We try to have a conditioned 11vs11, for instance, benefitting certain principles. Although training is not normally done over the entire field, focus on the intended principles, to bring out the principle of propensities (systemic repetition).

The level of concentration during the session is also more demanding, since the complexity of the drills increases. Due to this similarity to the reality mentioned previously, which together with increasing duration of the exercises, training should be as close as possible to the day of the competition.

Friday. Day of sub-dynamic speed.

We must begin the recovery (after the Thursday) for the next game to be played. Accordingly, we must work subprinciples of the game at every sector level, although we can also work at inter-sectorial or collective level, reducing the complexity of the game, and demanding levels of concentration that are lower than the previous day. We work with very little or no opposition and very small and intermittent training periods.

Oliveira (2006 mentioned by Gomes 2006) explains that, for this day, "the biggest concern is for the drills to have high speed decisions from the players, who are quick in decision-making and execution."

There is, therefore, a high speed of muscle contraction, which will make the drills short in duration and with no maximal tension. The number of repetitions must not be high.

It is, for example, about creating finishing situations without opposition, so there is high speed of execution. We must not confuse speed of execution with speed of movement. Another drill that works (as an example for this day) would be an 11vs11 game on a very small pitch, so we move the ball at very high speed.

Saturday. Active recovery and pre-activation for the game.

Saturday is all about pre-activation for the game on the next day. It is, as Oliveira (2006 mentioned by Gomes 2006) says, about "recovering from the previous days and activating the players for the game the day after, via very simple subprinciples." He says that he cares about "recalling certain aspects trained during the week but always without great effort… without opposition."

Concentration on this day must be relatively high but with low complexity drills (which generate sparse concentration). That is why the author works with "dynamic mechanization of the team, this is behaviors that do not demand much concentration but which remind everyone of collective patterns."

Since activation work is involved, there must be some speed and tension, but the duration must be reduced. This way we can work on completion exercises and recalling drills, etc.

Morphocycle Pattern with more than one game per week

"The Morphocycle Pattern will vary depending on the days available between competition." Frade (2005)

It must be clear that the morphocycle pattern will have variants, as we have said, one of the aspects to be taken into account when creating a morphocycle is the time available between one game and the next one, thus respecting the relationship between exertion and recovery.

In a morphocycle with two games, we should think about the recovery of the players, so it will vary its shape, without ceasing to meet the specificity that this process advocates.

For example

Game	Off	Recovery	Game	Recovery		Recovery	Game
Sunday	Monday	Tuesday	Game	Thursday	Friday	Saturday	Sunday

Graphic adapted from Oliveira.

Summary

The playing model guides principles and subprinciples. As players understand them better, they can be made more complex. In turn, principles and subprinciples can be modified depending on the needs of the moment or even prioritised over others.

The principle of specific horizontal alternation basically says there is a relationship between effort and recovery and that you do not change the tactical objective of a day (e.g. recovery), you change the components within that day (e.g. duration).

A sample week was shown above. It demonstrates how players are given time off following a game, and then build back up as the next game approaches. Whilst the level of physical activity and the focus of training might be reduced (as appropriate) intensity must not be allowed to drop. Players who did not take part in the previous game should be given more challenging work than those who did play.

The brain in the training process

"The learning capacity that defines human beings lies in the complex brain capacity we possess." Gaiteiro (2006)

Relation Brain – "Tactical Periodization"

"The aim will always be the same: to make rational the behavioral dynamic that is organization, philosophy, emotion. To create intentions and habits. To make a group of principles conscious and then subconscious in a way that we naturally display a certain way of playing." Faria (2006)

Throughout this book, we have seen that the brain plays a key role in our process of Tactical Periodization.

When talking about the playing model, we have linked it to a future vision, an image produced in our brain, an interpretation, that we must (through training) make as well-known as possible to the different individuals that form a team. Creating that "mental landscape" which Frade spoke about, understanding its wholeness, so we can later on link the parts with the whole (in its simplification).

We have also seen the importance of emotions and feelings (generated in the brain) in the process of anticipation; they reduce the brain processing/reasoning when we need to make a decision in similar or identical situations to the ones that we have already experienced. Anticipation that will help in the development of creativity so enjoys a privileged position in our process.

Tactical Periodization also emphasizes the assimilation of behaviors, not only at a "know how" level but also by

99

producing the relationship between "know how" and "knowing about know how." This is extremely important for specific concentration.

The importance of global understanding (game model) in the contextualization of the parts (principles and subprinciples),

"The mind is both artistic and scientific (Collins 2001), it is designed to understand and generate patterns to represent a constructed reality, but it resists the implementation of patters that make no sense or are enforced. The construction of those representation patterns requires the association of information that is stored and processed. So, when there is no possibility for this association, the representation patterns fail to acquire any meaning and become loose parts of information." Gaiteiro (2006)

The brain, as we know, consists of two hemispheres, the right hemisphere and the left one. "The left hemisphere rules the right side of the body while the right hemisphere commands the opposite side" (Israel 1995 mentioned by Gomes 2006).

Also, each hemisphere has a different type of processing. As Damásio (1994 mentioned by Gomes 2006) says, "in the left hemisphere prevails partial representations." and so, "it works in a logical and analytic way." To Laborit (1987 mentioned by Gomes 2006) "the right hemisphere, on the contrary, faces concepts and representations as a whole, this is, in its global aspect." However, even though "there is dominance of one of the hemispheres in the different brain functions... the brain works as a "whole." involving different areas, that are organized to perform the functions" (Gomes 2006).

This way, the right hemisphere, which is in charge of representing the whole body leaving the partial representation to the left hemisphere, will allow the representations of the left hemisphere to acquire a meaning and a more comprehensive perception, giving it a semantic organization (Gomes 2006).

This means that the understanding of the global representation (playing model) that happens in the right hemisphere of the brain, will allow us to understand, in a contextualized way, the partial representations (principles and subprinciples) that occur in the left hemisphere. In other words, the mental global representation, of the playing model, by the players, will enable the understanding of the principles and subprinciples, despite them being isolated during training, within that playing model. It will allow the players to understand and contextualize a part in the whole. That is why players must understand and know the playing model from the first day, so they can contextualize each of the trained principles and subprinciples.

To Gomes (2006), "The situations that are not inscribed in the playing model are abstract and do not promote a meaning in the information experienced in the process." Also, to the author, this understanding of the contextualized wholeness and its parts "stimulates the associative power of the representations." Representations etched in out memory, which will be used to "facilitate the interpretation" of the data of the context, it is no wonder that, as per Damásio (2003 mentioned by Gomes 2006), "The same object can provoke similar neural patterns." Gomes carries on and explains, "through this logic we understand that the way in which we see and interpret reality, that is, the context of exercising, results from the representations we own regarding that same context."

That is why it is so important to always work in a way contextualized to a playing model, as Tactical Periodization does. To Gomes (2006) "Under this this methodology,

a group of principles that develops familiarity with certain regularities is created and as a consequence, stimulates the ability to invoke representations that are associated to it." This will allow the ability of anticipation that has been addressed in this book.

Specificity that distorts the whole process

"People are obsessed with the physical aspect and only see the muscle as an organ that generates work and not as a sensible organ." Mourinho (mentioned by Oliveira 2006 referenced by Gomes 2006)

As per Damásio (1994) "The systems and circuits of the brain, as well as the operations that they carry out, depend on the connection pattern between neurons and the strength of the synapses that those connections create."

To the author, "the human genome does not specify the whole structure of the brain," but, "as we develop from infancy to adulthood, the design of the brain circuits that represent our developing body and its interaction with the world, seems to depend on the activities to which the body is engaged, and on the action of innate bio-regulatory circuits as the latter react to those activities." So, the experiences vary the strength of synapses, changing the design of the brain circuits.

Then, a certain way of 'playing' and its training process (as long as it is specific) will produce a completely different adjustment to another one, in this way modelling neuronal malleability. We are talking about a specific adaptation to all levels because, "brain and body are inseparably integrated through biochemical and neuronal circuits that connect each other" (Damásio 1994).

This adjustment may then be damaged by certain situations during training that are not specific to the intended way to play, causing "the neuronal networks to be altered because the players absorb (by the phenomenon of synaptic malleability) new stimuli and information that do not converge with what was developed. These exercises condition and disrupt the designed configuration of the training process" (Gomes 2006).

The same author explains it better with this example: "Let's imagine a process where the coach encourages situations which contribute to the principles of the intended playing model, however, after the training he tells the players to perform certain exercises using training machines. Through this situation, the coach alters the arrangements of the neuronal networks because the players absorb (by the phenomenon of synaptic malleability) new stimuli and information that do not converge with what was developed. These exercises condition and perturb the designed configuration of the training process."

That is why "Tactical Periodization" ceases to be "Tactical Periodization" when it is mixed with other methodologies, contrary to what many think.

Summary

Under Tactical Periodization, the playing model must be understood by all members of the team. Tactical Periodization seeks to educate and develop players into not just knowing what to do (know-how) but in understanding why (knowing about know-how).

Emotion is key to reducing a player's need to process information and make decisions. In doing this, players can anticipate events, and invoke actions more quickly. The brain is an amazing organ. It can make sense of isolated concepts, theories, principles and subprinciples and draw them together into a contextualized whole. This whole is the playing model which is why the different exercises and drills must always centre on the playing model, and players must understand the playing model clearly. In many ways, the brain will connect the dots.

The brain is 'plastic' in the sense that its structure changes according to the experiences a person goes through. These experiences vary the strength of the connections between neurons, literally changing the design of brain circuits. Thus, contextualized playing and training actually causes adaptation in the brain.

If training does not stay true to the playing model (i.e. exercises do not correspond to the playing model) then training can disrupt neuronal circuits hampering development and progression. Tactical Periodization ceases to be Tactical Periodization when it is mixed with other methodologies.

Chapter 12

The need to move football from the streets to football schools in response to its imminent disappearance

"In Football, education is important but this foundation can be formative and distorting. Good education is demanding and difficult." Frade (2005 mentioned by Fonseca 2006)

"The training process of a player is never finished." Fonseca (2006)

Talent: the genetic part and the trainee part

"Discovering talent is a complex art, the bad coaches and there are many) choose players based on size, weight, speed and all that that can be measured." Valdano (2001 mentioned by Fonseca 2006)

"Without talent in abstract, the recognition of talent implies reference tables, so the question is not how to detect talent, but to create settings where those talents can excel and evolve, in a way they will reveal themselves," Garganta (mentioned by Fonseca 2006)

As per Araujo (2004 mentioned by Fonseca 2006) "Talent is a concept that has been used to justify all that cannot be explained and which has something to do with the good performance of players."

There are many authors that give talent genetic values believing it is purely innate. However, "Genetics do not get to explain talent," (Fonseca 2006). To Garganta (2004 mentioned by Fonseca 2006) "To be a top player it is not enough to be born with talent, training becomes essential."

He added that, "before joining a training process, there may be talent, but the player only exists after training." So, "the innate, per se, is not enough to achieve excellence in football," Fonseca (2006), and adds (citing Araujo 2006) that, "We must promote certain contexts where there is a higher probability of talented interactions occurring."

It seems that, besides genetic issues, talented youngsters practice more than the rest, which explains why they reach a higher level of performance (Fonseca 2006). To the author, "the genetic perspective of the innate talent is clearly insufficient to explain the higher performance in the players." And adds that, "the quantity and quality of accumulated practice are revealed as essential" to become an elite player.

Street football: the real training school of world class players

"I spent my childhood playing football in my neighborhood in Porto Alegre, I never left the ball, and I dribbled, dribbled and dribbled nonstop. I played in the street with my friends, but I also played for hours just alone or with my dog, Bombom who was tireless. With him, I tried all possible dribbles, to avoid him catching the ball, except for the tunnel, because he had very short legs," Ronaldinho Gaúcho (in Pacheco 2005 mentioned by Fonseca 2006)

It is a fact, easy to confirm by looking through the window, that kids nowadays play less and less in the streets. Due to social development with the resultant increase in buildings, cars, and parks where playing football is forbidden… as well as an increase in school hours, kids have seen their playgrounds reduced.

Nowadays it is easier for them, and for their parents (and also less dangerous), to stay at home playing videogames or watching TV instead of going out and looking for a suitable and available place to play their games. This is something that has also affected street football. On few occasions, in more developed countries, do we see kids playing football in the streets.

In the past, and still today in most underdeveloped countries, the streets were full of kids that spent hours playing football. From those streets came most of the elite players as well as the most important players in football history (Maradona, Pelé, Eusebio, Ronaldinho…)

As per Ramos (2003 mentioned by Fonseca 2006) "The vast majority of elite players arrive at their clubs to form part of youth programmes (U-12, U-14, U-16, etc). This highlights the importance of the youth stages." What does this mean? It means that elite players do not get formed in the clubs, they get formed in the streets or lower level clubs, reaching high level clubs with the principal training already done. If so, we must ask ourselves what happens in this early training that does not happen in the training at high level clubs.

To Fonseca (2006) "That period that precedes admission to a club (street football) seems to be a fundamental part in the training process of elite players, being of extreme importance in the development of the different qualities of the player."

If this is so, and with the imminent disappearance of street football, we need to properly analyze the characteristics of good learning, to analyze the characteristics of street football for the importance it has shown in the development of elite players, and to transport these characteristics to football schools, which must assume the responsibility to link children to the game, in our case to football. Fonseca (2006) states, "In the face of an inevitable disappearance of street football, it is necessary that clubs and football schools import its matrix into their training process, with the aim of revitalizing that reality, using the corresponding recreational and educational potential."

Street football: a phenomenon that has the features of good learning

"Instead of regretting the fact, it is important to recognize and exploit the effervescence that makes that activity so rich in the conditions that promote the development of playing skills," Garganta (2006 mentioned by Fonseca 2006)

1. The contextualized and adaptive technique.

As per Calvo (2002 mentioned by Fonseca 2006) "Technique in football is one of the essential and key aspects to play well." However, even though "performing technical exercises is definitely necessary." "to practice them without a reference to the game makes no sense." because "kid needs a playing context before exercising technique," (Wein 1999 mentioned by Pacheco 2005 mentioned by Fonseca 2006).

To Wein (2006 mentioned by Fonseca 2006) "The teaching of football has been characterized by an excess of attention on the direction of the teacher/coach, frequently offering practices out of context to real game situations and with a lack of meaning for the player that gets bored by the constant repetition of a gesture and its limited transference." As per the author, "We try to improve a specific motor skill disconnected to the real situation of the game."

Also to Graça (1994 mentioned by Fonseca 2006) approaching the game through abstract techniques seems to be "a systematic error, once in the game, technical skills are almost always performed in situations of an unpredictable environment, where execution depends on the specific configurations in each moment of the game, imposing time and space for implementation."

As this abstract way to train technique is wrong, as raised by the authors, "In the process of teaching-learning, technique and tactics must be located in a single time, in other words, two sides of the same coin," (Mesquita, 2004 mentioned by Fonseca 2006). Technique in football must be an intelligent adjustment to the situations of the game, so, as we said in previous chapters, it is not about just teaching "know how" but to "know about that know how." We are talking about an adjustment of the technique to the different situations that may occur in the field. Adjustment that will be given by "knowing about a know how." as well as by experiences, according to Marina (1995 mentioned by Fonseca 2006) "even if it is impossible for the player to remember each of the exercises performed along the years of training, muscles do remember (…) practices and attempts are recorded in muscle memory…"

It is about creating training that adjusts technique to different possible scenarios. We must favour uncertainty, randomness and variability in the acquisition of technical skills, as well as the freedom response from the players, at the expense of abstract training that is closed and directed by the coach. As per Fonseca (2006) "To acquire flexible movements that are better suited to new situations or motor tasks, it is necessary to provide certain freedoms of response during the learning process, and to encourage players to explore their potential for movement… when that freedom is removed and we return to fully-directed learning, the emphasis is barely given to the invariable aspect of the skill, contributing to the formation of mechanized movement patterns of low adaptability."

Also, pretending to teach an "ideal motor pattern, common to all the players, this is the 'perfect technique' seems to be a fallacy, given the observed variability in the motor performance," Brisson & Alain (1996 mentioned by Fonseca 2006).

The adaptability of technique to different situations that we have been talking about, and which must take place together with the tactical aspect, is a characteristic of street football.

Adaptability in street football is given within a playing context, without any guidance by someone from the outside (coach) who provides the answers, but is the player himself who must adapt his motor patterns to the situation that the game demands in order to be efficient. The situation will differ every time due to the uncertainty and variability that comes with this sport.

2. Reduced, delayed and interrogative feedback.

There are two types of feedback: intrinsic feedback and extrinsic feedback. As per Schmidt & Franco (1993 and 2002 mentioned by Fonseca 2006) "the intrinsic one is the information obtained by sensorial and proprioceptive organs as a natural consequence of the execution of an action," while the extrinsic one is "additional information from external sources on the execution and outcome of the movement." (Fonseca 2006).

According to the authors, intrinsic feedback is, after practice, what promotes more and better learning of a skill. Also, as per Manoel (1989 mentioned by Ugrinowitsc 2003 mentioned by Fonseca 2006) "when the apprentice has lots of information about his execution, he cannot achieve a good performance,,, when there is a certain amount of uncertainty, the apprentice obtains a better performance in learning tests."

To Vickers (1999 mentioned by Fonseca 2006) "we must reduce and delay feedback so the players can solve the problem by themselves, once their performance is considered as acceptable by the coach." The author also claims that this reduction and delay of feedback "promotes self-confidence and less reliance on the coach." He also talks about the importance of this feedback being interrogative, so that it is the player who seeks and understands the mistake that has been made.

In street Football, feedback is usually intrinsic, since it is the player himself who realizes about the error that has been made, given the absence of a coach.

3. The existence of the error during learning.

According to Moreira (2000 mentioned by Fonseca 2006) "…man learns by correcting his mistakes, there being nothing wrong in making mistakes. It is wrong to think that certainty exists, that truth is absolute and knowledge is permanent."

The error is a feature that must be present during learning, because through errors we improve our actions, as well as storing actions in our memory that we must not perform; actions that will emerge in our mind ahead of certain situations, acting as a reference.

To Wein (2005 mentioned by Fonseca 2006) we must "create an atmosphere that is more tolerant to error, as happens in street football."

As Wein rightly says, in street football we learn when we make mistakes, by allowing personal learning from errors that are solved as a result of adjustments from the player himself, moving away from training processes where mistakes are punished, producing inhibition in the player, reducing or limiting their creative response. So we must try to guide the player, allowing him to be the one who learns from his mistakes, without prohibiting and punishing errors.

4. Playing as motivation.

To Wein (2003 mentioned by Fonseca 2006) "Playing is as important for a child as sleeping is, it is key for his physical health and for his mind. He learns when he is playing. This way he satisfies his desire to move and discover the world. Thereby, playing must always be a central point of each training session." Also, "Playing is the most important activity in order to keep children motivated and to help them to learn basic abilities of sport" (Knop, Côté, Baker & Abernethy, 2002 mentioned by Fonseca 2006).

So, playing stands out for its importance in the early ages, for its ability to develop the child physically, and mentally, and for its ability to create learning and to motivate.

Also Wein (2005 mentioned by Fonseca 2006) adds that, "we must encourage young players to create a game themselves, or to modify the rules of a suggested game," as this causes them to constantly adapt to new rules, forcing them to be creative.

5. A large amount of practice.

It is important to have a large amount of play, implying a large amount of practice for, as we have seen, hours of practice are a key factor in the training of elite players. For this number of hours to happen, it is essential to start playing football early.

To Frade (2005 mentioned by Fonseca 2006) "It is possible and wise to start very early." He assures that, "it is essential that feet and body are connected in the most diverse ways, so that coordination regarding the object that is not born with us is facilitated, because contrary to what happens with the relationship between the eyes and the hand, the relationship between the eyes and the foot is far more demanding, far more difficult, so the earlier the better." For him, "starting as early as possible is not a problem as long as the main activity is football," with "the ball always present." "It is key to assume the ball as a point of reference and a mandatory presence so that kids, from an early age, can relate to the game and the peculiarities of a certain football."

Fonseca (2006) explains that, "Starting early and, as a consequence, the amount of practice (game) hours accumulated, are necessary conditions in the training process of elite players, to reach higher levels of performance, even if they seem not to be enough, the quality of those practices is thought to be an important factor." So, even though quantity is necessary, it is essential that training is of quality.

The amount of practice that builds up in street football is much higher than that accumulated in football schools, which also tends to put more emphasis on working without the ball or out of context, and according to the authors this is wrong.

6. Pleasure as a learning booster.

The presence of pleasure appears to be an important factor in learning. To Fonseca (2006), "Without denying that learning without pleasure is possible, its presence seems to enhance and improve learning."

According to Damásio (2000 mentioned by Fonseca 2006) "People seek, consciously or unconsciously, feelings that cause them pleasure, turning away from feelings that bring pain or sadness. So, when feelings of pleasure are connected to certain actions/activities, these tend to be performed more frequently."

As we can see, the existence of the pleasure that occurs in street football may be one of the main reasons for its practice. That is why training must be enjoyable, something that actually occurs while we are playing.

7. Creativity at the service of order.

"Currently, most youngsters grow up in very hostile environments for the development of their creativity. Both family and school circumstances are typically characterized by a learning atmosphere of 'intentional orientation' (with strict rules), inhibiting individual initiative, independence and originality, in other words, trying in a different way."
Wein (2005 mentioned by Fonseca 2006)

There also seems to be, in the word of football, this rule of not permitting players to explore and do things differently;

this emphasises the process of teaching-learning in training, instead of encouraging creativity. According to Queiroz (1986 mentioned by Fonseca 2006) to improve this creativity we must rely on, "forms of playing where actions are developed with a certain degree of freedom."

Therefore, we must grant football with a certain disorder… we must promote creativity within some rules called principles and subprinciples that create an intended playing model. This creativity/detail will then be called subprinciples of the playing model.

To achieve this, we must work with exercises that promote problem solving, so we must be in charge of setting goals and the players will be responsible for creating ways to reach these goals; these exercises are a simulation of the game with the uncertainty that accompanies it. To Frade (2003 mentioned by Fonseca 2006) training is about drills where you "can 'inject' randomness, simulating self-organizing behaviors, in other words, using probabilistic processes instead of strictly deterministic ones."

Of course, street football allows this creativity, since there is no intervention by a coach, determining the action to be performed, allowing the detail to arise towards real game situations.

Training in football schools

"It is imperative for the clubs to think what the players have done from ages 5 and 6 until they are 14 years old, because, systematically, the players that stand out and then reach a higher level of performance in those clubs, arrive there when they are around 14 years old, and they come from a process without any concerns, where they play three times a week and then play in the streets. So we should only think about 'recycling' street football in order to create street football within those same clubs." Frade (mentioned by Fonseca 2006)

Having understood the importance that the matrix of street football has on the training of elite players, it is then our responsibility to try to 'import' those features into the training that takes place in our football schools.

This Training that we are talking about will then try to create players with tactical intelligence and the ability to adapt to the different situations that may arise, with a power of creativity that serves the playing model that the current coach advocates.

For this, in the first stages of training, individual development will be the focus, but also working collectively, players must have an idea of the 'intelligent organization' (a way of playing), adjusting their development to different situations. As they grow older, the organizational aspect will become increasingly important. However, this does not mean that the player will stop working individually, as per Fonseca (2006) "the training process of a player is never finished. This applies to all players, including the Elite ones."

Frade (2007) agrees with all this. According to the author, "Kids have many weaknesses that are circumstantial and one of them is the understanding of the collective." So, we must "worry about some situations where they are more collaborative and to me, this creates a perception that implies the understanding of a draft, a silhouette, something that eventually is an 'anarcho-gregarious' way of playing. He adds, "the priority is on the individual (individual growth) founded (supported) by cooperation." In other words, the utmost importance is given to the individual growth, without neglecting certain collective aspects.The author illustrates it as follows: "Street Football is 10 players (5 against 5) and that is what they must play, but in former days, Brazilians did not play the same football in the streets as the Scandinavians did, therefore not all football is the same."

So, even though there is a focus towards the individual growth during training, "if my concept is to advocate transversal lines or triangles, with a play of control and pass. I suggest games to the kids (3x3, 6x6 or 4x2) that suit this logic." creating an idea of play. However, I have to allow "individual growth in technical terms." The author explains that the notion of play "will only become a dominant concern in the future, especially from the ages of 14 or 15."

When observing and analyzing street football, to see that it meets the requirements that we are talking about, we must convey its essence to the way of training that we favour.

This way, we must create training sessions where the amount of contact with the ball is very high. A part of training must be with one ball per player. Normally this part is done during the warm up (it must be longer with beginners), where there are tasks of all kinds: dribbles, passes, controls, finishes... We must work with balls of all kinds (size, weight, material, shape). The use of bibs is not always necessary in drills, because it helps the player to recognize a partner without looking up, something that of course we are not interested in. Training will promote a way of organized playing, but without too much complexity (a draft). We must promote creativity and freedom so we must not limit the number of touches (something very common in all trainings), neither we should be constantly telling the players what to do.

A key aspect that we must not forget during the initial phases of training is the presence/existence of role-models (Zidane, Ronaldinho). In the teaching-learning process, the possibility of imitation cannot be absent, since one of the great difficulties with younger kids is abstraction, this is, the representation of the object in its absence. This visualization must be repeated consistently because one of the main principles of the teaching-learning process behind training is constant repetition that makes possible the acquisition of a "know how" or a "new know how." According to Frade, "It is necessary that the future will appear frequently in their eyes, so they imitate the future, and by imitating the future they get closer to it, sometimes even surpassing it."

We should not think that this type of training is only for youngsters. Despite the variation in goals, complexity, etc., all that we are talking about must also happen in adult groups (also in professional football), because even if more time is needed for developing a way of playing, we must continue working on the player individually for two clear reasons: the training of a player never ends, and (as we said in Chapter 5) in the absence of practice means that muscles forget . If we want quality football, we must promote this quality in our players, ensuring a high amount of time in contact with the ball.

To Frade, it is imperative to understand training according to higher performance and, the existence of a close link between the two of them. In other words, we cannot consider these two stages as unique and unrelated, instead we must think of them as the ends of a continuous process.

Summary

To become a top player, you need more than talent – you need to be trained, and it is the quantity and quality of accumulated practice that underpins elite players.

Street football used to be a breeding ground for successful footballers but due to modern living styles in developed countries, it has diminished considerably. Clubs would benefit from understanding what it is about street football that makes successful players and import its concepts.

Training technique is clearly important but it needs to be taught within a game-like context. As mentioned earlier in the book, players not only need know how, they need to know about know how. Whilst players might not remember all the exercises they performed across the years, muscle memory will.

Training is about letting players work out how to deal with different scenarios. Closed and directed instruction from the coach is not what happens when players learn in street football.

Intrinsic feedback is what the body 'tells' the player about an action (i.e. it is internal), extrinsic feedback is what third parties tell the player. Coaches should try to delay feedback so the players can solve problems by themselves. Man learns by correcting his mistakes, there being nothing wrong in making mistakes! Allow a player to be the one who learns from his mistakes, without prohibiting and punishing errors.

Playing the game develops a youngster mentally, physically and actually playing the game is the best motivation for any player.

Youngsters need a lot of practice and play to become elite, so get them started early. Make sure training is fun, we learn better when things are fun. Let players be creative, do not make training overly regimented, ordered or prescriptive.

With young players, the focus should be on developing the individual but support this through the co-operation of the team/organization.

Training should incorporate a lot of ball contact time. One ball per player is ideal with lots of different skills being worked. Do not limit the number of touches. The same principles should be applied across different ages and levels of the game.

Use role models as appropriate. Youngsters find it easier to connect with role model play/skills than with abstracted ideas or concepts. Bend it like Beckham, or jink like Ronaldo, for example!

Bibliography

Amieiro, N. (2005). Defesa à zona no Futebol. Um pretexto para reflectir sobre o <<jogar>>... bem, ganhando!. Porto. Monografía publicada.

Capra, F. La Condición Humana en la Alborada del Siglo XXI. Prospectos y Esperanzas. www.sgi.org

Carvalhal, C. (2001). No treino de futebol de rendimento superior. A recuperaçao é: muitíssimo mais que "recuperar." Braga. Monografía publicada.

Castelo, J. (1994). Modelo técnico-táctico do jogo. Ediçoes FMH. Lisboa.

Damásio, A. (1994-2006). El error de Descartes. Editorial Crítica. Drakontos bolsillo. Barcelona.

Damásio, A. (2003-2005). En busca de Spinoza. Neurobiología de la emoción y los sentimientos. Editorial Crítica. Barcelona.

Equipo Técnico de Psicólogos del Sevilla F.C. S.A.D., Universidad de Sevilla (España): Miguel Morilla Cabezas (coordinador), Eugenio Pérez Córdoba, Juan Manuel Gamito Manzano, Miguel Ángel Gómez Benítez, José Enrique Sánchez Loquiño y Mercedes Valiente Marín. Entrenamiento de la atención y concentración.

Una propuesta para fútbol. Revista Digital - Buenos Aires - Año 8 - N° 51 - Agosto de 2002. http://www.efdeportes.com/.

Faria, R. (2006). Presentación del libro: Mourinho: Porquê Tantas Vitórias?

Gradiva.

Fonseca, H. (2006). Futebol de rua, um fenómeno em vias de extinçao? Contributos e implecaçoes para a aprendizagem do Jogo. Porto. Monografía no publicada.

Frade, V. (1985). Alta competiçao no futebol – que exigências do tipo metodológico?. ISEF-UP. Porto.

Frade, V. (2003). Apuntes de clase FCDEF-UP.

Frade, V. (2005). Apuntes de clase FCDEF-UP.

Frade, V. (2007). Entrevista realizada por Lírio Alves.

Freitas, S. (2004). A especificidade que está na <<Concentraçao Táctica>> que está na ESPECIFICIDADE... no que deve ser uma operacionalizaçao da <<Periodizaçao Táctica>>. Porto. Monografía publicada.

Gaiteiro, B. (2006). A ciência oculta do sucesso! Mourinho aos olhos da ciência. Porto. Monografía no publicada.

Gomes, M. (2006). Do Pé como Técnica ao Pensamento Técnico dos Pés Dentro da Caixa Preta da Periodizaçao Táctica – um Estudo de Caso-. Porto. Monografía no publicada.

Garganta, J. (1996). Modelaçao da dimensao táctica de jogo de Futebol. Estratégia e Táctica nos jogos desportivos Colectivos. Centro de estudos dos Jogos Desportivos. J. Oliveira & Tavares, F. (eds). FCDEF-UP.

Garganta, J. (1997). Modelaçao táctica do jogo do Futebol – Estudo da organizaçao da fase ofensiva em equipas de alto rendimento. Tese de doutoramento. FCDEF-UP.

Gutiérrez, G. (2002). Claves de un nuevo paradigma para la Educación. Complejidad: Introducción, Metodología y dos ejercicios. www.udp.cl/humanasyeducación/psicología

Llauradó, J. (2003). Entrevista realizada por la página web del F.C. Barcelona el 6 de Junio de 2003.

Martins, F. (2003). A "Periodizaçao Táctica" segundo Vítor Frade: Mais do que um conceito, uma forma de estar e de reflectir o futebol. Porto. Monografía no publicada.

Moriello, S. (2003). Sistemas complejos, caos y vida artificial. Moriello, S.A. Copyright 2003 REDcientífica. http://www.redcientifica.com/

Morin, E. (1984), (1985), (1990), (1999), (2001). www.edgarmorin.org

Morin, E. (1984). Ciencia con consciencia. Pensamiento crítico/Pensamiento utópico. Barcelona. Anthropos. Editorial del hombre.

Morin, E. (1990). Introduçao ao Pensamento Complexo. Publicaçoes Europa – América. Lisboa.

Oliveira, B., Amieiro, N., Resende, N. y Barreto, R. (2006). Mourinho: Porquê Tantas Vitórias?. Gradiva. Lisboa.

Oliveira, J. (1991). Especificidade, o "pós-futebol" do "pre-futebol." Un factor condicionante do alto rendimento desportivo. Porto. Monografía no publicada.

Oliveira, J. (2003). Entrevista In Tavares. Uma noçao fundamental: a Especificidade. O como investigar a ordem das "coisas" do jogar, uma espécie de invariância de tipo fractal. Porto. Monografía no publicada.

Oliveira, J. (2007). Procesos de Formación de Jóvenes Futbolistas con Talento. Construcción de un Sistema/Modelo de Juego y su respectivo análisis. Dibujos o Esquemas del Morfociclo Patrón. Presentación ofrecida por el Profesor Guilherme Oliveira.

Portolés, J. (2007). Entrevista realizada por Xavier Tamarit.

Portolés, J. (2006). Apuntes de Master en Alto Rendimiento.

Vega, R. (2003). Principales consideraciones acerca del entrenamiento de la concentración en el fútbol. Revista

Digital - Buenos Aires - Año 9 - N° 60 - Mayo de 2003. http://www.efdeportes.com/

Resende, N. (2002). Periodizaçao Táctica. Uma concepçao metodológica que é uma consequência trivial (da especificidade do nosso) jogo de futebol. Um estudo de caso ao microciclo padrao do escalao sénior do Futebol Clube do Porto. Porto. Monografía no publicada.

Rocha, F. (2000). Modelo(s) de Jogo/Modelo(s) de Preparaçao – "Duas faces da mesma moeda." Um imperativo conceptometodológico no processo de treino de equipas de rendimento superior?. Porto. Monografía no publicada.

Schuster, B. (2007). En una entrevista realizada para el diario As el Martes 4 de Septiembre de 2007

Tavares, J. (2003). Uma noçao fundamental: a Especificidade. O como investigar a ordem das "coisas" do jogar, uma espécie de invariância de tipo fractal. Porto. Monografía no publicada.

Tena, Luis Fdo. (2006). Artículo del entrenador del América de México en el diario As el 14 de diciembre de 2006.

Wikipedia (2007). es.wikipedia.org

Zambrotta (2007). Articulo del jugador del F.C. Barcelona en el diario Súper Deporte el 19 de enero de 2007.

Bennion Kearny Soccer Books

The Modern Soccer Coach by Gary Curneen

Aimed at Soccer coaches of all levels and with players of all ages and abilities The Modern Soccer Coach 2014 identifies the areas that must be targeted by coaches who want to maximize a team's potential – the Technical, Tactical, Physical, and Mental sides to the game. See how the game has changed and what areas determine success in the game today. Learn what sets coaches like Mourinho, Klopp, Rodgers, and Guardiola apart from the rest. Philosophies and training methods from the most forward thinking coaches in the game today are presented, along with guidelines on creating a modern environment for readers' teams. This book is not about old school methodologies – it is about creating a culture of excellence that gets the very best from players. Contains more than 30 illustrated exercises that focus on tactical, technical, mental, and physical elements of the game.

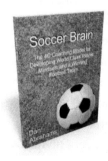

Soccer Brain by Dan Abrahams

Coaching soccer is demanding. Impossible to perfect, it requires a broad knowledge of many performance areas including technique, tactics, psychology and the social aspects of human development. The first two components are covered in detail in many texts – but

Soccer Brain uniquely offers a comprehensive guide to developing the latter two – player mindsets and winning teams.

Soccer Brain is for the no limits coach. It's for the coach who is passionate about developing players and building a winning team. This is not a traditional soccer coaching book filled with drills or tactics or playing patterns. This book is about getting the very best from you, the coach, and helping you develop a coaching culture of excellence and world class football mindsets.

 **Soccer Tough: Simple Football Psychology Techniques to Improve Your Game** by Dan Abrahams

"Take a minute to slip into the mind of one of the world's greatest soccer players and imagine a stadium around you. Picture a performance under the lights and mentally play the perfect game."

Technique, speed and tactical execution are crucial components of winning soccer, but it is mental toughness that marks out the very best players – the ability to play when pressure is highest, the opposition is strongest, and fear is greatest. Top players and coaches understand the importance of sport psychology in soccer but how do you actually train your mind to become the best player you can be? Soccer Tough demystifies this crucial side of the game and offers practical techniques that will enable soccer players of all abilities to actively develop focus, energy, and confidence. Soccer Tough will help banish the fear, mistakes, and mental limits that holds players back.

The Way Forward: Solutions to England's Football Failings
by Matthew Whitehouse

English football is in a state of crisis. It has been almost 50 years since England made the final of a major championship and the national sides, at all levels, continue to disappoint and underperform. Yet no-one appears to know how to improve the situation. In his acclaimed book, The Way Forward, football coach Matthew Whitehouse examines the causes of English football's decline and offers a number of areas where change and improvement need to be implemented immediately. With a keen focus and passion for youth development and improved coaching he explains that no single fix can overcome current difficulties and that a multi-pronged strategy is needed. If we wish to improve the standards of players in England then we must address the issues in schools, the grassroots, and academies, as well as looking at the constraints of the Premier League and English FA.

Scientific Approaches to Goalkeeping in Football: A practical perspective on the most unique position in sport by Andy Elleray

Do you coach goalkeepers and want to help them realise their fullest potential? Are you a goalkeeper looking to reach the top of your game? Then search no further and dive into this dedicated goalkeeping resource. Written by goalkeeping guru Andy Elleray this book offers a fresh and innovative approach to goalkeeping in football. With a particular emphasis on the development of young goalkeepers, it sheds light on training, player development, match performances, and player analysis. Utilising his own experiences Andy shows the reader various approaches, systems and exercises that will enable goalkeepers to train effectively and appropriately to bring out the very best in them.

Developing the Modern Footballer through Futsal by Michael Skubala and Seth Burkett

Aimed at coaches of all levels and ages, Developing the Modern Footballer through Futsal is a concise and practical book that provides an easy-to-understand and comprehensive guide to the ways in which futsal can be used as a development tool for football. From defending and attacking to transitional play and goalkeeping, this book provides something for everyone and aims to get you up-and-running fast.

Over 50 detailed sessions are provided, with each one related to specific football scenarios and detailing how performance in these scenarios can be improved through futsal. From gegenpressing to innovative creative play under pressure, this book outlines how futsal can be used to develop a wide range of football-specific skills, giving your players the edge.

The Footballer's Journey: real-world advice on becoming and remaining a professional footballer by Dean Caslake and Guy Branston

Many youngsters dream of becoming a professional footballer. But football is a highly competitive world where only a handful will succeed. Many aspiring soccer players don't know exactly what to expect, or what is required, to make the transition from the amateur world to the 'bright lights' in front of thousands of fans. The Footballer's Journey maps out the footballer's path with candid insight and no-nonsense advice. It examines the reality of becoming a footballer including the odds of 'making it', how academies really work, the importance of attitude and mindset, and even the value of having a backup plan if things don't quite work out.

Making The Ball Roll: A Complete Guide to Youth Football for the Aspiring Soccer Coach by Ray Power

Making the Ball Roll is the ultimate complete guide to coaching youth soccer.

This focused and easy-to-understand book details training practices and tactics, and goes on to show you how to help young players achieve peak performance through tactical preparation, communication, psychology, and age-specific considerations. Each chapter covers, in detail, a separate aspect of coaching to give you, the football coach, a broad understanding of youth soccer development. Each topic is brought to life by the stories of real coaches working with real players. Never before has such a comprehensive guide to coaching soccer been found in the one place. If you are a new coach, or just trying to improve your work with players - and looking to invest in your future - this is a must-read book!

 **Universality | The Blueprint for Soccer's New Era: How Germany and Pep Guardiola are showing us the Future Football Game** by Matthew Whitehouse

The game of soccer is constantly in flux; new ideas, philosophies and tactics mould the present and shape the future. In this book, Matthew Whitehouse – acclaimed author of The Way Forward: Solutions to England's Football Failings - looks in-depth at the past decade of the game, taking the reader on a journey into football's evolution. Examining the key changes that have occurred since the turn of the century, right up to the present, the book looks at the evolution of tactics, coaching, and position-specific play. They have led us to this moment: to the rise of universality. Universality | The Blueprint For Soccer's New Era is a voyage into football, as well as a lesson for coaches, players and fans who seek to know and anticipate where the game of the future is heading.

Soccer Tactics 2014: What The World Cup Taught Us by Ray Power

World Cups throw up unique tactical variations. Countries and football cultures from around the globe converge, in one place, to battle it out for world soccer supremacy. The 2014 World Cup in Brazil was no different, arguably throwing up tactical differences like never seen at a competition in modern times. Contests are not just won by strong work ethics and technical brilliance, but by tactical discipline, fluidity, effective strategies, and (even) unique national traits. Soccer Tactics 2014 analyses the intricacies of modern international systems, through the lens of matches in Brazil. Covering formations, game plans, key playing positions, and individuals who bring football tactics to life - the book offers analysis and insights for soccer coaches, football players, and fans the world over. The book sheds light on where football tactics currently stand… and where they are going. Includes analysis of group matches, knock out stages, and the final.

Coaching Psychological Skills in Youth Football: Developing The 5Cs by Chris Harwood and Richard Anderson

Written specifically for soccer coaches of all levels, Coaching Psychological Skills in Youth Football details the 5Cs of Commitment, Communication, Concentration, Control, and Confidence in a methodical and practical manner with real-world exercises for training and matches. The book is relevant to soccer coaches working with 5-16 year old players, with individual techniques and practices marked for appropriate age groups. By weaving these techniques into their normal coaching practice, coaches will help educate young players to optimise their motivation, discipline, composure, self-belief and teamwork. A complete 12 month development plan is included alongside a case study from a youth coach who has actually experienced the 5C journey.

The Modern Soccer Coach: Position-Specific Training by Gary Curneen

Aimed at football coaches of all levels, and players of all ages and abilities, The Modern Soccer Coach: Position-Specific Training seeks to identify, develop, and enhance the skills and functions of the modern soccer player whatever their position and role on the pitch.

This book offers unique insight into how to develop an elite program that can both improve players and win games. Filled with practical no-nonsense explanations, focused player drills, and more than 40 illustrated soccer templates, this book will help you – the modern coach - to create a coaching environment that will take your players to the next level.

Printed by BoD™in Norderstedt, Germany